BEING

A JESUS FOLLOWER'S INTRODUCTORY GUIDE

INTERCULTURAL

TO NAVIGATING CULTURE WELL

STEPHEN W. JONES

Citations from the Bible are from the Contemporary English Version unless otherwise noted.

Copyright © 2015 Stephen W. Jones

Cover design by Marcus Dip Silas

Interior design and graphics by Josiah Enns, Stephen W. Jones, and Marcus Dip Silas

ISBN-13: 978-1-940105-50-5

Published by

Viscereality Intercultural Development Corporation

Omaha, Nebraska

http://www.thepracticalinterculturalist.com

http://www.viscereality.us

CONTENTS

ACTIVITIES

Big Ideas

An unfortunate side effect of a title like "Being Intercultural" (which I think does capture the goal of the book well) is that it might imply that I, the author, have somehow attained some exalted status to which I am now calling my readers. Certainly I am very much still on the journey myself. However, it seemed that this potential misunderstanding of the title was worth risking because the idea of *Being Intercultuaral* speaks to a more central truth. Relating interculturally is not something that one can merely do. It is not the sort of thing which you can check off a list. Neither is it a simple thing. Effective relating across cultures is the sort of journey that necessarily involves transformation in perspectives.

At times, learning to deeply understand the lived experiences of others can invite us into a perspective transformation that is really challenging. I have attempted to deal with some of the reasons why this is so in Unit 5 and as well as in another recent book entitled *Social Constructivism and Christianity*. The challenge of bringing together truth and culture can lead to significant mental and even spiritual discomfort. As I have come to know followers of Jesus from many different cultures, however, I am increasingly convinced that God is not in anyway intimidated by these differences. Furthermore, it seems that He delights in revealing Himself as complex and complexly knowable.

MOTIVATION AND SPIRIT-EMPOWERMENT

If we pursue intercultural competence with goals like profit, which through proper application it can help generate or increase, then I suppose we can say with Jesus that we "have had our reward". But if instead the endeavor of building intercultural competence is engaged from a perspective of love, a different world of resources and rewards opens up to us. We can engage the pursuit of intercultural competence based in our love for Christ, in our love for the brethren, and in love for the world that He loved so much that He gave up his own life in order to facilitate the restoration of our broken relationship with Him.

As we pursue being motivated by love, intercultural competence becomes one more avenue through which we can be "transformed through the renewing of [our] minds" (Romans 12:2 ESV). Or as the CEV puts it, "let God change the way you think." Moreover, as we pursue intercultural competence from the perspective of love, we find that His own Spirit is already at work in us, granting discernment and wisdom, even prompting us to will and to work for His good pleasure that we may shine as lights in the world (Phil 2:13-14). Of course, one of the great things about the Spirit at work in us is that He is not limited by our intercultural incompetence. And yet this is a tool we can use as we walk wisely, and certainly it pays dividends both in relationships within the church and with demonstration of the values of Heaven on earth.

IS IT ACADEMIC?

This book is not a particularly academic one. My fellow interculturalists may be disappointed with the lack of research included here or the lack of detailed analysis of the cultural continua and other concepts presented herein. On the one hand, that critique is a legitimate one. When I use this material in class, I use it alongside more academic presentations, such as that offered by Martin (one of my MA profs) and Nakayama.

However, I encourage you not to mistake the lack of the academic for a lack of relevancy. Indeed, the goal of this book is to bring the intercultural perspective into focus – to make it accessible and practical. For some, this will naturally and appropriately lead to a more detailed academic and research-based study of culture, from which we all stand to benefit. But there are some, the front-line practitioners of the world, as it were, who need to comprehend this information experientially more than they need to know it cognitively. This book is intended to help both sets. Indeed, I hope that the Concrete Experiencer, the Abstract Conceptualizer, the Reflective Observer, and the Active Experimenter (*a la* Kolb) each find their own resonance with the material herein.

MOVING FORWARD TOGETHER

It is my hope that this edition of this book is a beginning, more than a culmination. It is offered as a movement of conversation - much like Muneo Yoshikawa seeks movement from both interactional parties in the performance of the dynamic-in betweenness of intercultural exchange, this work is more like an opening overture in what I hope is an ongoing co-creation between academics, theologians, intercultural practitioners, and the church at large.

Acknowledgements begin on the next page, but it seems appropriate to stop and thank the reader for your willingness and interest in pursuing this journey. Thank you in advance for your feedback, and thank you for caring.

Stephen W. Jones
August 2015

ACKNOWLEDGEMENTS

THANK YOU FOR THE JOURNEY

We've already lost track of exactly when it was, but some years ago Garrett Swanberg and I were sitting in the Burger King on South 13th Street in Omaha catching up about life when something he asked prompted me to explain some of the basic insights of the intercultural perspective. I drew out a basic sketch of Bennett's Development Model of Intercultural Sensitivity on the back of the tray liner and was delighted not only that Garrett immediately comprehended the model, but that he also saw the incredible relevance of this perspective in his work with Release Ministries, which works with high-risk youth in the Omaha area.

That impromptu meeting led to training opportunities that eventually led us to develop a written curriculum for the intercultural training of the staff. Release, in my view, leads the way in terms of urban and youth ministries that *get* intercultural training. This became abundantly clear when Garrett suggested that Release does not only want their staff to become interculturally competent, but that their real goal is to help their clients use the intercultural perspective as a way to navigate "the system" while maintaining their own cultural identities. Those familiar with urban and high-risk youth work should recognize that this is a radical position – equipping youth to succeed in majority culture society while also equipping them to succeed in their home culture. Too often, youth are forced to choose one or the other.

The book you now hold in your hands has been developed from that original curriculum that Garrett and I developed with the sharpening brought about by the practical and intense feedback and requirements from staff serving in Homes, Mentoring, and Community Based Initiatives. I expect that as our relationship continues, the input from Release will continue to lead to more and more practical iterations of the material presented here in future editions of the book. In gratitude for their leadership, a portion of the proceeds from each book is donated to Release Ministries.

I have also had the privilege to journey for some years now with the Evangelical Protestant Church of Mali, and particularly with my friends Rev. Joseph Camara and Marthe Diallo and Mama Sacko and Susanne Coulibaly. So much of what I have experienced with moving from theory to practice has been accomplished while in relationship with you. Thank you for your ongoing friendship. Thank you Dr. Youssouf Demebele for the wisdom you imparted to my students and the willingness to share in Kingdom work. Thanks to Pastors Marka Diarra, Levi Coulibaly, Noumongolo Sogoba and Imanuel Diarra and your families for your friendship and the conversations over the years. They have shaped and reshaped the ways in which I understand the church.

Thanks to "Big John" Perkins, who walked with me through some hard times as we looked to move theory about reconciliation in the church into practice. I am grateful for your continued friendship.

Thanks to Rev. Dwight Ford, who invited me into the African American community in Omaha and helped me to see the richness and complexity there. Our time together there was shorter than we had hoped, but what we had was rich.

Many thanks to the Christians in Mexico who helped to shape my early understanding of intercultural relations. To those who were students and professors at Puebla Bible Seminary when I was there in 2003, thank you for your patience and for your willingness to invite me and my fellow students into your lives and ministry. Thank you to the pastor whose name I don't know but who helped me to understand the challenges brought about by intercultural incompetence among missionaries.

Thanks to Mike, Tiffany, Rebecca, Sharon, Todd, Rachel, Beth, LaVern, Isabelle, Joseph (again), Nanga, and others who have been on the journey at the intersection of life and faith that we call Life Shared International.

Thanks to Randy Burg, David Manske, and David Manfred and your families for helping to restore my faith in the majority culture American church after it had been seriously depleted. Thank you for smelling like Jesus (2 Cor. 2:14-15).

Thanks to David Hof for inviting me into the relationship between UNK and Pine Ridge; even though I was not with you long, I see ways in which the work we did together have shaped me.

Thanks to Geraldine Stirtz for your deep commitment to service-learning and to my family. You helped to guide us through a difficult but very formative time. Jennie and I are grateful for your friendship.

Thank you to all my in-laws in Central Nebraska who continue to love us even though we're unpredictable. Thank you for helping me to understand the rural American experience as complex and rich. Thank you for your steadfastness in Christ. Thank you for pouring into our children.

Thanks to Jeannie and Steven who keep me connected to the military experience and whose friendship I value. We enjoy doing life with you guys.

The above list is too short, but stands for the many who have been part of the journey of helping me to see the beauties in the complex cultural differences of this world.

THANK YOU FOR THE INPUT

Thanks to my profs at the Intercultural Communication Institute's MA in Intercultural Relations program and to authors who have gone before me in the Intercultural Field. I hope I have represented your theories well while navigating the intersection of faith and culture and that I have given appropriate credit where it is do. I offer my sincere apologies for any mis- or missed-representations.

THANK YOU FOR THE HELP

Many thanks also to the many individuals whose direct and indirect support have made this book a possibility. Special thanks to Marcus Dip Silas and Josiah Enns for your contributions. Thanks also to my students for testing and sharpening a lot of this material as we worked through transitioning it to a more general audience. Thanks to Dad and Uncle Jack for looking through the manuscript.

THANK YOU FOR EVERYTHING

Finally, it seems a little cliché to include this in the acknowledgements, but it is true. I am grateful to God for the opportunity to live at the intersection of faith and culture - what a fun and rewarding place to be. Tremendous thanks also to Jennie and to my kids, it's a privilege to do life with you.

INTRODUCTION

WELCOME TO THE JOURNEY

As a follower of Jesus in the 21st Century, you live in an exciting time. At the same time that Christianity is flourishing among more peoples than at any time in human history there is also an intense global diaspora of many different people groups. It is increasingly possible for people from all walks of life to rub shoulders with those who look different, eat different foods, and speak different languages. We have witnessed the transformation from intercultural competence being the exclusive need of a few professionals to this skill set being a main-stream necessity.

This book is a response to that reality – a reality where many Christians find themselves routinely faced with difference, but often also find themselves under-equipped for engaging in really successful interactions across cultures. While this book does celebrate the fact that there are Christians in many different people groups, this is not a book that dwells on multiculturalism. The multicultural movement (if it can be called that) and its associated trainings, often emphasize an almost Pollyanna, excessively optimistic, view of culture. Many of us have sat in trainings where people have suggested that if only we can learn to recognize that we are all the same, then we can get along. That idea is nice, but it is simply insufficient.

This book, then, does not take a multiculturalist view that all people are simply the same and that we just have to recognize that sameness. Instead, it takes a rather more complicated tack and holds competing realities in tension. Here are a few foundational principles held by this book:

* All people are equally valuable because each is an image bearer of God (Gen 1:27).

* Culture is a concept we use to describe the patterns demonstrated by groups of people – culture is not a thing.

* In part because culture is not a thing, no culture is inherently good or evil – every human culture has capacity for both good and evil.

* Jesus is capable of and desires to redeem people from every human culture (John 12:32, 2 Peter 3:9, Romans 10:11).

* Every culture reflects certain truths about God, though often in different ways.(Acts 11:1-18, Romans 1:18-21. Romans 2:14-15)

* Every culture reflects the fallen nature of humanity, though often in different ways (Acts 11:1-18, Romans 1: 18-2:16, 11:17-24).

* Despite certain fundamental similarities, people are capable of being *very* different from each other.

Because of these complex truths, this book does not intend to convince you that all conflict will be resolved simply by recognizing our shared humanity. On the contrary, this book invites you on a journey of discovery of both fundamental similarity *and* difference. While there is much to celebrate in our human cultural differences, the reality is that it is often difficult to navigate those differences well. Anyone who tells you otherwise likely does not really understand just how differently people can perceive the world from each other.

This book is a journey of discovery. This journey might be unsettling, but you can trust that this is a journey that is also rooted in a fundamentally monotheistic and Christocentric understanding of reality.

GOSPEL TRUTH THROUGH CULTURE

As followers of Jesus we are committed to Jesus Christ, to the Word of God, and to the Christian Church. The **relationship with God** that we desire to see transform society comes through personal encounters with Jesus. Our cross-cultural life and work must be motivated out of our relationship with Christ if it is to be fully effective. No amount of training in professional or cultural competence can replace the power of adoption (Romans 8:15, Ephesians 1:5) that believers have in the family of God.

It is out of this relationship with Christ, from a stance of being adopted into the family of the King, from a recognition of the deep human need for Jesus, that we are able to live transformative lives in society.

As those who are adopted, we are no longer required to demonstrate our worth to the King, to the Kingdom, or to society. You and I no longer have to earn our place based on our merit, but are instead freed to do the life work to which we have been called (Ephesians 2:8-10). We no longer have to defend ourselves (1 John 2:1). We no longer have to strive to provide for our basic needs (Matthew 6:25-34). All of this is settled by the work of Jesus in our lives. He promises that the Father will provide what we actually need. He declares us righteous (Romans 5:19, 2 Corinthians 5:21, 1 John 2:2) in spite of our sinfulness. He declares us clean because He alone can cleanse us (Acts 15:9).

That Jesus has settled these needs on our behalf frees us to love (1 John 4:19). It frees us to love Him, to love our neighbors, and even to love ourselves (Matthew 22:36-40). We are freed to be inspired to serve Him fully. Ephesians 2:8-10 paints the picture (ESV):

> *...by grace you have been saved through faith. And this is not your own doing; it is the gift of God, not a result of works, so that no one may boast. For we are his workmanship, created in Christ Jesus for good works, which God prepared beforehand, that we should walk in them.*

The needs of our communities and nation are great, and the setting is complex. Through building intercultural competence, we will be better equipped to accurately understand and relate to the cultures not of only our non-Christian neighbors, but also of your fellow brothers and sisters in Christ (1 John 3:14). Your intercultural competence journey will also help you to better serve even people who are culturally similar to you.

THE GOAL OF THIS BOOK

This book seeks to fill a special void – specifically, although there many books written on intercultural competence, most of those are focused on business people, college students, or missionaries. What's more, many of those books have the goal of just helping the reader develop in their ability to relate across cultures.

This book is different. Originally written in partnership with Release Ministries, which serves high-risk youth in Omaha, this book was designed not only to help you to develop your own intercultural competence, but to go beyond this in preparing you to develop intercultural competence in others so that they can better engage their own environment – whether that is in a rural church, an inner-city ministry, or your corporate setting.

WHO THIS BOOK IS FOR

This book is intended primarily for American Christians coming from multiple ethnic backgrounds. The style generally follows dominant American cultural patterns while recognizing important contributions of other groups. Readers from some backgrounds may find some of the examples and language more difficult to understand, but the general principles still apply. If you do find that there are elements that do not make sense to you, feel free to contact us at www.thepracticalinterculturalist.com to let us know!

This book is written for people who engage cultural difference in any number of life circumstances: at work, in the church, at home, at the grocery store, in local organizations, in local government and in the school. Whether you are a ministry leader or a layperson, or even if those distinctions are irrelevant to you, we trust that you will find this book helpful. We also invite your suggestions on how to make the book more accessible to people like you, so please feel free to share suggestions with us!

HOW TO USE THIS BOOK

This book is intended to be used in several different ways:

1. As a supplemental textbook for introductory intercultural courses

2. As an independent, self-paced reader/workbook

3. In guided independent work, where you meet with a supervisor or coach to discuss important / assigned topics

4. Together with a group

5. As part of a training session or event

ABOUT ACTIVITIES

Most activities can be accomplished within this book, but some do involve stepping away to read another book, watch a clip or film, or to go do observations of some kind in a public location. After you have completed the activity or done the external reading, I highly recommended that you take advantage of the reflection / analysis space in this book to make a note of the main lessons you have learned. That will make this book more useful to you in the long term, as you can come back here and reference the most important takeaway lessons you encountered in those other sources. There are also several recommended activities that require a qualified administrator, such as the Intercultural Development Inventory. Special instructions are provided on how to access those kinds of resources.

ABOUT "AT THE INTERSECTION"

Scattered throughout the book are stories entitled "At The Intersection" that highlight the interactions that happen as people from different cultures relate to each other. All of these stories are based on real intercultural interactions or elements from real interactions. Some are told from a perspective that may be culturally similar to your own, while others may be told from a perspective that is culturally dissimilar to your own. If you find, when reading one of these stories, that you are not sure "what the point" is, try applying the various cultural frameworks presented in the book to analyze the story from another perspective.

ABOUT THE INTENTION OF THIS BOOK

As was mentioned previously, this book is intended not only to guide you toward developing intercultural competence. It is also intended to lead you through a process of developing certain basic competencies that will help you to teach others how to use these lessons for their own benefit. As you go through any activity, remember to consider it both from your own perspective and from the perspectives of those you serve and work with.

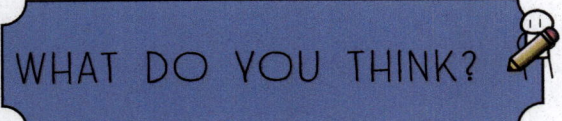

WHAT DO YOU THINK?

As you think about beginning this journey of intercultural learning, what is on your mind?

What do you hope to accomplish using the insights you want to gain from this book?

AT THE INTERSECTION

When Steve was in fourth grade, his family moved from Japan to California to Kansas. In spite of only receiving about four months of actual fourth grade education, he experienced a lot in that year. Yet experiencing is not the same as learning, and much of what Steve had experienced in fourth grade did not make sense to him until he was in graduate school, studying intercultural relations. Over and over, he would stumble across some insight that shed light on a little more of what he had experienced during that year of beautiful chaos.

TOPIC ONE: INTRODUCTION TO CULTURE

As you begin this journey of intercultural learning, it is important that we create a framework in which you can really learn as you experience the various activities in this book. Depending on your own life experience, you might even be asking yourself why you need to know about culture. The short answer is that **culture** is everywhere, and it influences how we understand everything. A simple way to say it is this:

Culture is how people do their stuff together.

Consider how culture forms: People all have needs that they have to meet in order to stay alive. For example, how do we eat? What do we drink? What kind of shelter do we have? All of these kinds of questions have to be answered, and since people are generally social, we usually answer these questions together.

But it is not just about these kinds of physical questions. People also have to figure out how to communicate with each other. How do we know when our relationship is ok? How do we know when we are fighting? How do we solve conflicts?

One of the surprising things about culture is that because we grow up in a culture, we often do not notice that these decisions are being made. For many of us, we just live life as normal. But every day we make more decisions – we are "*culture-making*" all the time.

At The Intersection

Maria grew up in an American inner city area. His parents intentionally relocated to a poorer part of town before he was born. Maria attended a church that had a multiethnic congregation and formed good friendships with many people who were of many different ethnicities. Due to diverse influence in his life, Maria grew up experiencing multiple cultures. In his college years, he was able to form relationships across multiple cultures. People enjoyed Maria's genuine interest and ability to adapt to the cultures that he interacted with. Maria also showed a keen sensitivity in dealing with cross cultural conflict. He was often the mediator between conflicts that occurred in the dorms between his friends of different cultural backgrounds. Maria continues to maintain and cultivate new friendships with people who are different than him.

Because we simultaneously 1) grow up in a culture (that is called **enculturation**) and 2) help form our culture, it can be hard to recognize its effects around us. This first section of the book will help you develop a basic understanding of culture, through two sections.

In this first topic, **Introduction to Culture**, we explore where culture is, how culture can be seen, ways to describe cultural patterns, and the inescapability of culture.

In the second topic, **Awareness of Culture,** we draw awareness to judgments we subconsciously make every day, how those judgments are culturally biased, and how the rules of culture are largely unspoken.

Big Idea #1: Culture is Everywhere

As mentioned before, culture is a way to describe the patterns around how people do their stuff together. Anywhere there is a group of people, that group has to determine how to live life. We can think about this on many different levels. Let's start close to home:

Activity 1.1 | Family Culture

In a family, what kind of decisions do people have to make that form patterns for life? Make a list of daily-life tasks that have to be accomplished for a family to survive:

example: providing food for the family

If you are working through this activity with a group, compare the ways in which you answered the above question. A topic that often arises in this activity is the recognition that even the idea of what "survival" is for a family can vary widely.

As a family goes about answering the questions of what needs to be done and who does what, certain expectations become standard for the family. Circle two of the items in the list above, and describe the pattern that your family has (or had) to make sure that the task was completed.

e.g.: **mother purchased food once a week from list. Breakfast was cereal with milk, everyone packed his/her own lunch for the day, and mother cooked the evening meal. The exception was Sunday, when father cooked the noon meal.**

If you are working with a group, compare your answers.

As you can see, even in the most basic questions of life, certain patterns emerge around how we, as humans, choose to live. Although there are other ways to think about the formation of cultural patterns, for now we will look at the ways in which these decisions form the basis of culture. Once these decisions have been made, they are often perpetuated through teaching and learning, which ensures that the practices are continued.

Eventually, beliefs develop to support the teaching and learning of these practices, until they become such a normal part of life that they become "common sense," and we forget that we ever made a decision in the first place!

Decision:
How we do life

Supporting Beliefs

Becomes Common Sense

WHAT DO YOU THINK?

What other patterns can you think of that have come from decisions people made? Think about the way in which your business or school functions, the way your local, state, and national governments function, the borders of countries, or even your neighborhood's demographic composition.

 **Discover More!**

 Follow the link at left to read about how Americans made decisions that resulted in concentrated urban poverty, but then largely forgot about those decisions and began to consider the massive concentration of poverty – and especially poverty among non-White residents – as a normal, common sense aspect of American life, rather than one that resulted from a specific set of decisions.

AT THE INTERSECTION

Matt and his wife, Carlene, are former missionaries to a South East Asian country. After 7 years abroad, they moved back to the United States to be closer to family. Both Matt and Carlene have a huge heart for immigrants and upon their return, they began reaching out to an immigrant community close to their home. Due to previous experiences, this particular immigrant community is not too fond of outsiders. However, when the community perceived Matt and Carlene's endeavors to be genuine, they began to open up. Not too long after, Matt and Carlene began to receive invitations to participate in celebrations that were usually reserved for family, such as coming of age celebrations and high school graduations. Many of Matt and Carlene's friends were surprised at the openness of the immigrant community toward them as this community was not known to be friendly to outsiders. The couple continue to foster good relationships with the community and are even considered honorary elders by the youth within the community.

VALUES

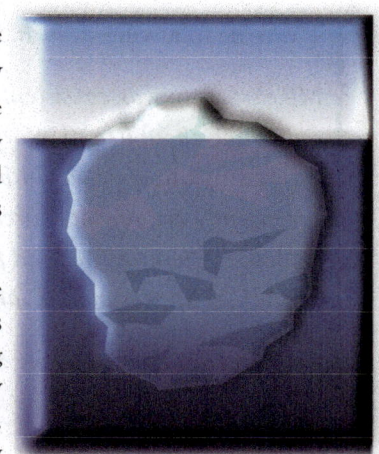

Another important factor in the development of culture is **values**. Values sometimes guide the way in which life decisions are made, and at other times result from the need to firmly establish those decisions. Although **beliefs** are similar to values, values differ in that they are held subconsciously. Values may be considered to be unquestioned assumptions about how life works, and may both incorporate and inform religious, philosophical, and other related beliefs. One of the keys about values is that people generally cannot identify their own values unless they come into contact with a competing value.

One of the ways that culture is often described is using the metaphor of an iceberg, because the majority of an iceberg is not visible above the waterline. Like any metaphor, this one has its limitations (in this case, because culture is much more of a process than a thing). Proceeding with this metaphor despite its difficulties, the elements of culture that we can most easily identify are behaviors – those familiar expression of culture related to how people dress, eat, interact, and so on. Beliefs are much more difficult to see, but we can understand that they directly undergird and relate to behaviors, and people are often able to explain their beliefs when asked. Much more obscure are the deeply held values – which may easily be overlooked or ignored because they do not seem related to the behaviors. However, values are some of the most important keys to understanding behavior.

Again, as we use this simile it is important to recall that culture is not static, and neither does its existence necessarily threaten the passerby who interacts with it. However, this understanding of culture does allow us to draw a few important observations.

* First, as with an iceberg, there is much more than "meets the eye". Thus, casual or short-term encounters with people from another culture will not enable you to really deeply understand a culture.

* Second, in a similar way to how the lower portion of an iceberg allows the upper portion to be visible through providing the buoyancy necessary to lift it above the water's surface, the beliefs and values in a culture, although not readily apparent, tend to support the behaviors of a culture. Thus, any attempt at change agentry within a culture must recognize that the change of behavioral patterns alone may be ineffective at generating long-term and comprehensive change.

* Third, icebergs are not static. They move and shift in response to the dynamic environment in which they exist. Recognizing the limitations of the metaphor here, we nonetheless see a parallel in that cultures change significantly over time – and this change is especially accelerated as cultures "bump into each other".

* Finally, the hidden elements of icebergs, like the hidden elements of culture, can be studied. Once the presence of these underlying aspects have been discovered, they may be (with considerable effort) explored and studied.

 **Discover More!**

 Follow this link to learn more about the limitations of the iceberg metaphor. Using the culture as an iceberg metaphor, let's return to the idea of family as one of the core 'culture-makers' in the next activity:

ACTIVITY 1.2 | SEEING VALUES, BELIEFS, AND BEHAVIORS IN FAMILY CULTURE

Read the following story and identify the values, beliefs, and behaviors, as well as their development in the family culture.

Mike's family was consistently late for church, arriving around 5 minutes late each week. His parents decided to do something about it, and informed Mike and his sister Sheila that they would no longer be late for church. If the kids made the family late, they would be fined a dollar per minute out of their allowance. Within several weeks, the family was consistently arriving at church five minutes early. Mike and Sheila began to harass their friends who were late to church, explaining that this was bad form. Years later, when one of Mike's employees showed up late to work, Mike lectured him about how 'time is money,' and warned that this irresponsible behavior would not be tolerated at the company.

In this story, what decisions were made about behaviors?

What beliefs were developed in response to those decisions?

What values (underlying assumptions) were never questioned?

Discerning the values in this story may be difficult. The primary value at play relates to the nature of time. In the present example, the family utilizes a **monochronic** approach to time, in which time is a limited, linear, resource. If you share this approach, it may be very difficult for you to see this value. There are other values at play here, but if you can see the time one, that's a great start!

WHAT DO YOU THINK?

Have you ever had an argument with someone where you just couldn't seem to understand each other?

Could it be that the problem was that you actually had different deeply held values?

BIG IDEA #2: CULTURE HAS MANY DIFFERENT LEVELS

If we are going to use culture as a way to understand the world, one of the important things that we have to know is that everyone is a participant in multiple cultures at the same time. Every person shares certain values, beliefs, and behaviors of more than one cultural group. This is again one of the reasons why it is important not to think of culture as a "thing" but more as a process in which people participate. Both the cultural patterns shared by groups, as well as the individual experience of and identification with culture are dynamic. Consider the multiple cultural 'layers' that Norah interacts with in the following story.

ACTIVITY 1.3 | LAYERS OF CULTURE

Norah is an engineering student at a state college in a medium-sized city in Nebraska (about half a million people). She attends a local Christian church (evangelical) on the weekends when she isn't traveling home to visit her family in Kansas. They live on a small cattle ranch outside a town of about 1200 people. Norah's boyfriend Adam is from Seattle. He is studying international agricultural law. He became interested in the field after seeing his father (who emigrated from Brazil) negotiate successful deals for multi-national companies. Adam returns home for three months each summer to help his younger brothers, who have struggled significantly since their mother (an African American woman) passed away. Adam is especially concerned for his older brother Steve, who is currently homeless. With the help of Adam's dad, Norah's older sister Megan is planning to move to Seattle with her girlfriend after she and Megan get married, which is a secret that Norah has promised to keep from her Catholic parents. Adam teases Norah about being the only Korean living on a ranch in north-central Kansas. She doesn't mind, because she really identifies with her white adoptive parents and feels very comfortable in her home community.

First, identify what surprised you as you were reading. Go back and put a little star next to each item that surprised you.

Second, identify the cultures mentioned in this brief biography about Norah. List all types of cultures mentioned with the appropriate person:

Norah

Adam

Norah's Parents

Adam's Dad

Adam's Mom

Steve

Adam's other Brother(s)

Megan

As this story illustrates, people's experience of culture can be incredibly complex. We often don't realize how many cultures overlap in any given person, and we may not realize some of the layers even after knowing someone for years!

Here are a few layers of cultures to consider:

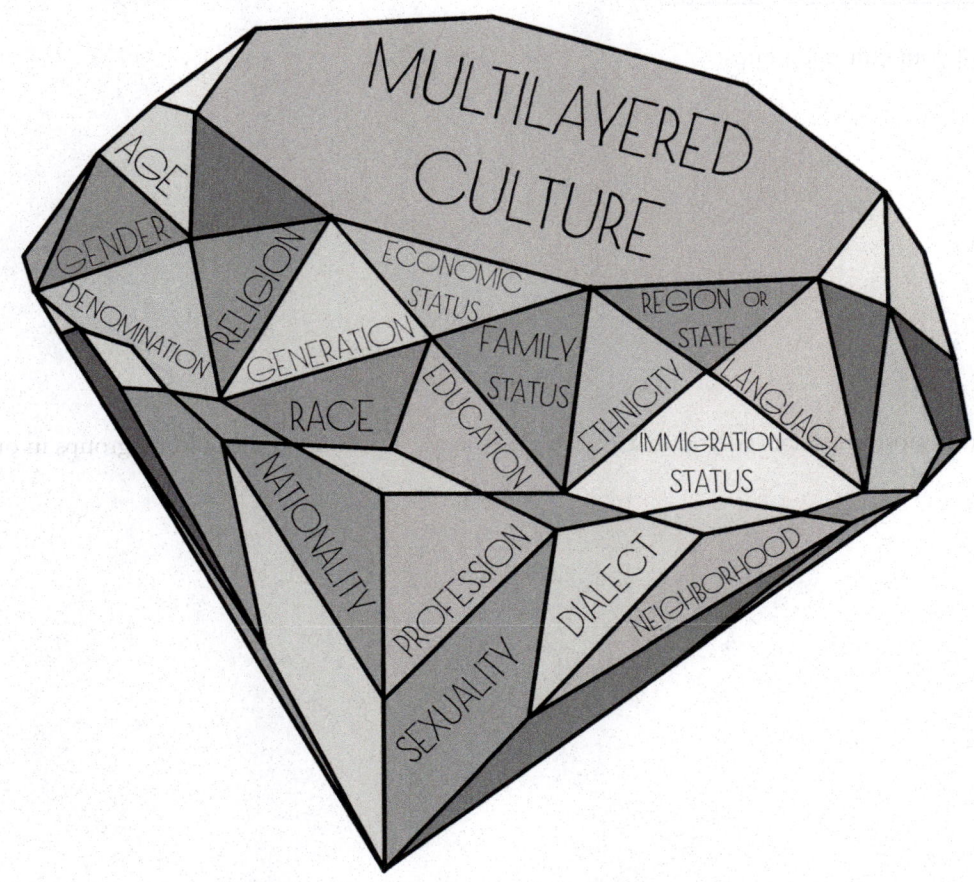

AT THE INTERSECTION

Alice had a hard time fitting into her freshman year at a Christian liberal arts college. She had taken two years off after graduating high school to work at a preschool. While working, she enrolled herself in a local community college. She worked a full time job while taking night classes three times a week. She began her time at the Christian college, expecting to be a sophomore. However, she was told that only one of her course credits had transferred and she would start as a freshman. Beyond this frustration she did not feel like she connected with most of her dorm mates. Her roommate was four years younger than she was and was a junior by credits because of AP courses she had taken while in high school. One night, Alice's RA reprimanded her for using a swear word in a dorm Bible study. Alice was taken aback because the word she had used was part of most people's daily vocabulary where she grew up. Alice felt frustrated and disappointed but she could not figure out why.

Try to make a list of your cultural groups:

In which cultures is it most important to you that you're a member? Try ranking the cultural groups in order of importance to you.

Discover More!

Follow this link to hear Pico Iyer discuss the complexities of participating in multiple cultural groups at once.

BIG IDEA #3: YOU CAN DESCRIBE CULTURE WITHOUT BEING RACIST

You probably already understand that we should avoid **stereotypes**. What is sometimes less clear is what exactly stereotypes are and why we should avoid them. When using culture as a lens to understand people's behavior and interactions, it is important to know how to address tendencies in various cultures without stereotyping.

ACTIVITY 1.4 | IDENTIFYING STEREOTYPES

Which of the following would you consider to be stereotypes? Check the box for each line that you think has a stereotype.

- ☐ Asians are good at math.
- ☐ Mexicans are lazy.
- ☐ Mexicans are good workers.
- ☐ You just can't trust African Americans, they're too violent.
- ☐ If you're tall and black, you are a good basketball player.
- ☐ White people are just rich and lazy. They always make everyone else do the hard work.
- ☐ Poor people are always working the system – you know, welfare moms.
- ☐ People growing lots of food in their yards are pot-loving hippies.

One of the problems with stereotypes is that they often contain some nugget of truth – it may be truth that has been misperceived, but nonetheless there is usually something that the stereotype user is basing the statement on.

How to identify stereotypes:

- ❋ Stereotypes are rigid and inflexible.
- ❋ Stereotypes are broad.
- ❋ Stereotypes are applied to everyone in a particular group.
- ❋ Stereotypes are usually, but not always, negative.

As you can tell from this list, *all* of the items listed above can be classified as stereotypes. Even positive stereotypes can have negative consequences. For example, according to stereotype 1, Asians are good at math. How might this stereotype affect you if you were an Asian who did not excel at math?

GENERALIZATIONS

While it is clear that stereotypes do not enhance our understanding of people from different cultures, it is often necessary to speak about tendencies within groups. To do this, we use **generalizations**. Some features of generalizations:

1. Generalizations speak about general tendencies.

2. Generalizations are not expected to fit any given individual.

3. Generalizations are tentative, used as open hypothesis.

4. Generalizations use limiters like "tend to", "often", and "in general".

5. Generalization are best used as judgment-free statements.

To see the difference between generalizations and stereotypes, it may be helpful to picture these visually:

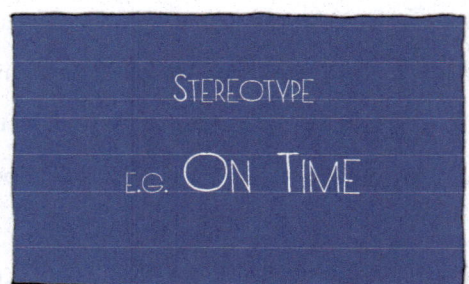

AT THE INTERSECTION

Damian remembered having a happy childhood. His father worked as a construction worker and his mother worked shifts at a local grocery store. Money was often tight but his parents taught him how to be content with what he had. His parents were very intentional about instilling good values into Damian and his siblings. Damian loved to read and spent a lot of time at the library when he was growing up. He preferred a good book over playing sports and was a Mathlete during his high school years. Damian graduated an honor student from his high school and pursued an education in engineering at a well-respected state university. One night, at a student mixer hosted by his RA, he struck up a conversation with another freshman named Emily. When Damian recounted where he was from and his major, Emily expressed her surprise. She exclaimed that she did not know people like Damian enjoyed academic related activities. She embarrassingly admitted that her first impression of Damian had been to assume that he was an athlete. After Emily walked away, Damian reflected on the encounter and was unhappy that she had based her first impression of Damian on a stereotype.

As you can see, in stereotypes, lines are clearly drawn between group A and group B. In generalizations, you can expect that the tendencies of population A will overlap somewhat with those of population B. At the same time, you can accurately use a generalization to say "People in group A *tend* to be direct communicators, while people in group B *tend* to be indirect communicators," for example. Finding an individual who doesn't fit this pattern is not a threat to the generalization. The generalization does not have to threaten the individual, because it is simply referring to the tendency of the group, not of any particular individual within the group.

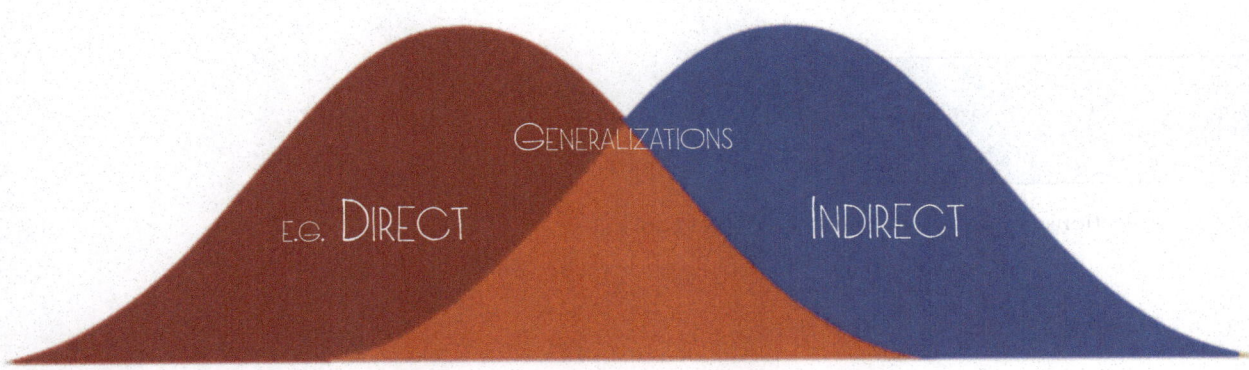

AT THE INTERSECTION

Max was adopted by American parents when he was 12. Growing up, Max developed a love for the arts. His parents encouraged his interests by sending him to music and drawing classes. Max excelled in the arts and enrolled in a music degree program. Max disliked mathematics immensely and often struggled with subjects that involved numbers and calculations. After flunking his College Algebra test for the second time, his teacher called Max to her office and expressed her disappointment with Max. Max was told that he should excel at algebra since *his people* were supposed to be really good with mathematics. Max left his teacher's office puzzled. What did she mean by his people? Having grown up in a middle class, mostly white, American neighborhood, Max identified more with the dominant culture than the culture of his country of origin, and he didn't know whether the people from his original country were unusually good at math anyway.

Big Idea #4: You have a culture

 **Discover More!**

Find a book or video that talks about your culture. Here is a recommendation to get you started:

 *American Ways: A Cultural Guide to the United States of America 3rd Edition. By Gary Althen, and Janet Bennett. Boston, MA: Intercultural Press, 2011*

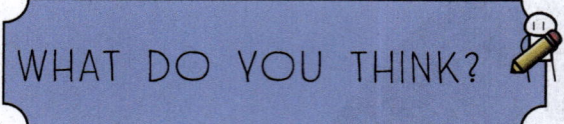 WHAT DO YOU THINK?

Jot down your reflections as you read the American Ways book.

What do you agree with?

What do you disagree with?

TOPIC TWO: AWARENESS OF CULTURE

In Topic One, we considered the ideas that 1) **culture is experienced everywhere** and involves self-reinforcing patterns, 2) **culture is experienced at many different levels** and thus every person has a complex cultural identity, and 3) that we can **describe cultural patterns through generalizations**. We ended that topic with the idea that you have a culture', and you had the opportunity to consider your relationship to American culture through reading and reflection.

The rest of this workbook is designed to help you apply these basic ideas practically as you relate to other people, including both their similarities and differences.

Topic two presents an exploration of the ways in which culture influences everyday life and interactions. This is especially important to understand, because of the foundational role it plays in your future intercultural success – whether internationally or at home. Because of the foundational importance of this section, be sure to push into the reflections.

BIG IDEA #5: WE SUBCONSCIOUSLY JUDGE EVERY INTERACTION

One of the first steps in honest intercultural communication is recognizing that we actively **judge every interaction we have with other people**. In any interaction, there are two primary channels of communication.

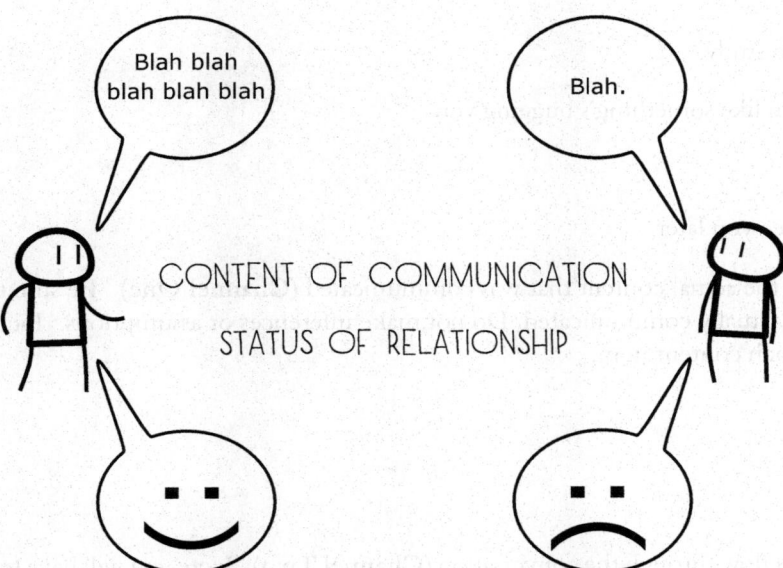

Both of these channels are communicated through verbal and nonverbal signals, and each culture has its own rules for how this content is packaged.

The important takeaway here is that in every interaction with another human being, you are likely to be both sending and receiving information on both of these channels, whether or not you are consciously aware of it.

ACTIVITY 1.5 | DISCOVERING TWO CHANNELS OF COMMUNICATION

Read the following interaction and watch for communication on Channel One and Channel Two. Use the numbers to identify movements in the interaction.

1. Peter: Hi Don! How was your weekend?

2. Don: Oh, hey Peter. It was ok.

3. Peter: Oh, man, what happened? Did you go on that date with Sue?

4. Don: Yeah, we went out. It was cool.

5. Peter: That's good.

6. Don: Yep.

7. Peter: So that's it?

8. Don: Yeah. I'm gonna go study.

9. Peter: Hey man, you seem like something's bugging you.

10. Don: No, I'm fine.

11. Peter: Whatever dude. See you later.

First, make a list of what was the actual content that was communicated (**Channel One**). Be sure that you do not include any information that was not actually communicated. Do not make inferences or assumptions. Include the line number of the conversation to back up each content item.

Second, describe the relational flow through the conversation (**Channel Two**). Here you will have to make some inferences. Again, back up your answers with the line number.

Third, if you are working through this book with others, compare your results with your group. Especially look for differences in the ways that you interpreted Channel Two information. What similarities and differences did you find? Do you have any ideas about why you interpreted some of these things differently from each other?

If you are working through the book alone, try to see if there are other ways in which a person could understand the conversation. For example, how might your impression of the conversation change if you found out that Don had just found out that his mother had cancer?

AT THE INTERSECTION

Daniel and Malcolm were college housemates during Daniel's senior year. They had been friends for three years, with Malcolm being a year Daniel's junior. Initially, Daniel had been really excited to live with Malcolm because Malcolm was a friendly and well-liked student. On move-in day, Daniel's family came to help Daniel move in. Having already moved in, Malcolm was at the door to greet them. After being introduced to Daniel's family, Malcolm immediately instructed Daniel and his family to remove their shoes before entering the carpeted house. Daniel was puzzled and stated that it would more practical to have their shoes on as they were going in and out of the house. Malcolm insisted that no shoes were to be worn indoors at any time. Daniel reluctantly complied and shook off the incident as a one-time deal. As the days grew into weeks and into months, Daniel began to grow weary of Malcolm and his weird lifestyle habits. He decided that people only liked Malcolm because they did not know who he truly was. One day, Daniel could not take it anymore and blew up at Malcolm. From that day on, Malcolm gave Daniel the cold shoulder. Daniel could not understand how Malcolm could be so well-liked when he was such a difficult person to live with. When Daniel graduated, he was relieved that he would be moving out. On the day when Daniel's family helped him move out, Malcolm just sat on the couch looking at his phone. Daniel and his family similarly ignored Malcolm as they removed Daniel's belongings with their shoes on the entire time.

As humans, we are constantly involved with evaluating and judging interactions with other people. We weigh the available information to come up with judgments about:

1. Trustworthiness / Integrity of the person we are interacting with

2. Competence of the person we are interacting with

3. Status of our relationship with the person we're talking with

4. The relative authority between ourselves and the person we are interacting with

5. The moral character of our communication partner

What may be surprising about the prevalence of our judgments in interactions is that we do this **constantly**. It doesn't matter whether we are interacting with our best friend, the car salesman, a religious leader, or the clerk at the gas station, we are constantly making these kinds of judgments. While these judgements are often accurate, they are sometimes inaccurate. However for the moment, your goal is not primarily to determine whether these judgments are correct or incorrect. Instead:

GOAL: One of our goals in intercultural communication is **learning to recognize the judgments we make in every interaction.**

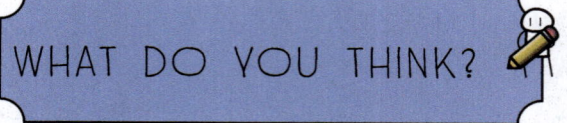

Can you think of an example of a time when you misjudged an interaction with someone? What happened?

Why might it be good to practice seeing the judgments you make when interacting with others?

Do you know someone who has ever made inaccurate judgments in their interaction with others?

BIG IDEA #6: WE TEND TO BE BIASED TOWARD OUR OWN CULTURE

If we are constantly making judgments in communication, it is important to consider the criteria by which we make those judgments. You may be surprised to know that we actually make snap-judgments of people we interact with (or even just pass-by on the street) based on information we gather in a fraction of a second. While some of these judgments can be remarkably accurate, some are downright wrong.

 **Discover More!**

For more on this, look into thin-slice judgments, based on the work of Dr. Nalini Ambady:

 *http://ambadylab.stanford.edu/pubs_thinslice.html*

It is not possible to stop making snap-judgments. For example, when you flipped to this page, you probably formed some kind of subconscious opinion about the character (or at least mood) of the people pictured here:

Photo Attributions: Marcus Dip Silas

ACTIVITY 1.6 | IDENTIFYING SNAP JUDGMENTS:

Briefly write down your initial impressions of the three faces pictured above. There is no right or wrong answer – the goal is to recognize what your brain has already done upon viewing these images.

Now ask yourself these questions:

If I was at a park with my younger sister, and something happened to me, which one of these men would I prefer to have look after my sister until my parents got there?

Why?

What you may or may not be aware of is the **subconscious track at play in your brain**. When you interact with another person, your brain immediately tries to look for familiar features. One of the key questions your brain will ask is 'safe' vs. 'unsafe'. Because there are so many variations in people's appearance and behavior, you have to rely on certain "scripts" to tell you whether a person belongs in the safe or unsafe category.

One of the key elements of safe vs. unsafe is (usually) familiarity. Of course, in abusive situations this script does not work in the same way. However, in general, the more familiar a face is, and the more familiar nonverbal behavior is, the more likely a person is to be put into the familiar, safe category.

ACTIVITY 1.7 | WHAT MAKES A "SAFE PERSON"?

Briefly think through what attributes you might assume are safe or unsafe and place them on the continuum below. These can include things like height, skin tone, expression, vocal styling, how close someone stands to you, touching during communication (i.e. hand on shoulder / arm), tone or pitch of voice, gender, language, presence of body art (piercing / tattoos), perceived hygiene, body odor (or other odor), wrinkled vs. smooth skin, directness vs. indirectness, etc.

If you are working with others, compare your answers with the group. If you are working alone, explain why you put the different elements where you did. Why do certain attributes seem safer or less safe?

There are **relative levels of familiarity**, which are accessed depending on who else is present in a given situation. For example, in a situation where most of the people are of the same age and ethnicity (i.e. a junior high dance in a mostly white Midwestern town), people might group around differences such as gender (such as boys in one area and girls in another).

In a situation where a person cannot find people with very many similarities (such as when traveling internationally) sometimes the only criteria for trustworthiness is that a person speaks the same language as you. For example, it is not uncommon to see travelers look for help in fellow travelers based solely on the passport they were carrying, even when it is highly unlikely those same people would have interacted favorably while in their home country due to other differences.

The key takeaway here is that at a really basic level **we are always judging whether other people are 'safe' or 'unsafe,'** and that the perceived degree of similarity (usually) increases the perceived "safeness" of another person. On the other hand, the perceived degree of difference (usually) increases the perceived "unsafeness" of another person.

WHAT DO YOU THINK?

Can you think of a time where you pre-judged on external attributes and later found out you were wrong?

Why might the human tendency to make snap judgments be good for you to be aware of?

BIG IDEA #7: IN THE GAME OF INTERCULTURAL INTERACTIONS, THE RULES ARE LARGELY HIDDEN

In everyday interactions, there are unwritten rules that govern successful communication. See if you can answer these:

In a conversation, who looks away first, the speaker or the listener?

Which of the following distances should you generally stand from someone when having a conversation?

> 6 inches
> 18 inches
> 3 feet
> 5 feet

When visiting someone's house, who initiates saying goodbye, the visitor or the host?

Every culture has its own answers to these kinds of questions. For example, in majority American culture, the speaker often looks away first, people tend to stand about 18 inches apart, and the visitor tends to initiate a goodbye. A firm handshake along with a smile and direct eye-contact will tend to lead to better results among majority culture American men than a limp handshake, a non-emotive face, and the avoidance of eye-contact. However, there are cultures in which this is exactly the opposite!

The first goal here is to begin to **recognize that many of our 'common sense' behaviors are based on unwritten rules.** Our second task is to recognize that the reason that **we know the rules is because we were taught them as part of our enculturation** (the process of growing up in a culture).

ACTIVITY 1.8 | PRACTICE SEEING CULTURAL RULES

This activity borrows from the practice of **ethnography**, a tool used by cultural anthropologists to learn more about a culture.

Take this book or a notebook to a place where you can watch people interact with each other for a long time – at least an hour, but preferably for several hours. Malls, coffee shops, downtowns, and some bars are good places to sit and observe.

As you observe people, answer these questions:

1.   How are you feeling? Your own feelings will change the way you interact with what you see, so it is a good habit to record how you are feeling as you begin.

2.   How do people dress here? Do a certain groups of people dress differently from each other? Does dress seem to impact how people interact with each other?

3.   How do people relate to another? What is the noise level like? Is the noise level different between generations (if there are multiple generations present)? What do "couples" do in public? How do families or people of mixed gender interact?

4.   How do people get around (cars, walking, public transportation, etc)?

5.   What kind of interactions do people have with technology? Who has what kinds of technology with them?

AT THE INTERSECTION

After a few years at an American college, Luke, who was an international student, developed feelings for a new student named Kelly. Unlike Luke, Kelly grew up on a farm in a small rural town. After a couple of months of getting to know each other, Luke asked Kelly out on a date. They discussed expectations and the changing dynamics of their friendship. After a couple of dates, Kelly decided that she was not ready for a relationship after all and she tried to break it softly to Luke. Even though Kelly was not ready to commit to an exclusive relationship, she requested that they continue their friendship as before. Luke agreed to this and promised to not avoid Kelly. He began to initiate group hangouts with Kelly and her friends. Kelly thought this to be a little odd, but went along because she enjoyed hanging out with Luke. As time continued, Kelly felt like Luke was more and more involved in her life and she started to get confused about whether or not he was trying to get her to like him. However, she was not sure what to do did not express her concerns to Luke.

Meanwhile, Luke was content. Even though a romantic relationship had not worked out, he very much enjoyed having Kelly as a big part of his life. He had made good on his promise to not avoid Kelly and he had decided to arrange group hangouts so that he could still hang out with her without making her feel awkward. One day, Kelly had had too much of the ambiguity in their relationship. She confronted Luke over a text and accused him of manipulating his way into her life even though she had clearly said that she was not ready to commit to a serious relationship. She told Luke that she did not trust his intentions and told him to stop sending her mixed signals. Luke was devastated and hurt by what Kelly had to say. He stopped all communication with Kelly and considered the friendship as a loss.

6. How do people interact with each other? Who is with whom? Who is alone? Who doesn't interact with whom? Who avoids whom?

7. How do people greet one another? How do they say goodbye?

8. What other observations have you made?

This activity is often a lot of fun. What you may have discovered is that there are actually a lot of patterns of interaction that we take for granted. One of the important lessons from this activity is that **although these cultural rules are mostly unwritten, we can often discover them through careful observation.**

Look for the cultural insiders – because the cultural rules are usually unwritten, people within a given culture will think that those rules are just "common sense." Sometimes you can find a cultural insider who understands the rules well enough to explain them to you, which can be really helpful. However, be aware that the first people you make contact with in another culture may be marginal to their own culture. People that are well established in their own cultural milieu are generally not looking for outsiders to interact with. So, as you look for cultural insiders to give you insight, be sure to test their perspectives before assuming that they necessarily represent the cultural group you are learning about.

BIG IDEA #8: WE USE OUR UNWRITTEN RULES TO JUDGE OTHERS

If you recall that **many of people's 'common sense' behaviors are based on unwritten rules**, and if you understand that **you were taught those rules as you grew up,** then it may not be surprising to know that…

> *Other people often have different "common sense" rules that cause them to behave differently from us.*
>
> *When we apply our unwritten rules to everyone equally, we sometimes misinterpret other people's words and actions.*

One of the most challenging results of this is the recognition that "treating everyone the same" can actually be one of the most **unfair** things we can do!

The following activity explores the ways in which we apply common sense rules in the family context.

ACTIVITY 1.9 | CASE STUDY: APPLYING COMMON SENSE RULES

John's family was pretty normal as far as he could tell. Here are a few things about his family:

1. He and his brothers enjoyed playing outside in the dirt, and they especially loved to find frogs and snakes. They didn't have a lot of money, so their mom was happy to encourage this inexpensive entertainment. She would help them create little homes for the creatures using boxes with air holes. Not wanting to miss an opportunity for educating her boys, they would go to the library to find books about the creatures and study all they could about them.

2. Sunday was a big day for their family with church obligations, but it was also supposed to be a day of rest. So, the dinner on Sunday nights was particularly light: apples and popcorn. Although this didn't satisfy the boys' hunger, they were used to the pattern and rarely complained. For some reason their dad would often visit the neighbors on Sunday night, who found that it was a great time to grill steaks.

3. The family would dispose of every kind of trash in the garbage. They didn't keep a messy house, but with several boys around, it wasn't ever completely clean. Various items seemed to mysteriously move around the house as the boys would pick up items of interest and deposit them along their way as they walked.

One summer John's family was looking for a house they could afford. This had stretched on longer than they had expected, and they accepted the hospitality of some friends from church, who invited them to live with them as they looked for housing. Here are a few things about the hosting family:

1. The family did not have children or pets, and kept the house very clean and tidy. Everything had its own place, and was expected to stay there.

2. The family had a strong sense of pride, and even when they were financially tight would go to great lengths to keep up appearances. They were much quicker to give help than to receive it, feeling that being in someone else's debt was a situation to avoid.

3. The family had come from a rural background and was accustomed to burning their trash. They thus disposed of most of their trash by burning it, being careful to set aside items such as shaving cream cans, which would explode in the fire.

Despite the best intentions of both families, as you might imagine there were certain conflicts that arose over time. Initially, both families were able to ignore the differences, focusing instead on their friendship. But over time, the goodwill was replaced by tension.

What kinds of judgments do you think the families made about each other?

There were two events that set things over the edge. First, as you might have anticipated, the hostess stumbled across one of the snakes living in a shoebox in the garage. It frightened her so much that she knocked over the box, releasing the snake into the house. The second event was equally unfortunate. Not knowing that the family burned their trash, John's dad threw his rusting shaving cream can into the garbage with the intention of keeping the house clean. Again, as you might have guessed, this trash was burned in the fireplace. The can exploded (this was before the days of safety pressure releases) and shot burning trash all over the host family's living room. Fortunately they were able to extinguish the flames, but not before a ring of fire had permanently damaged the carpet. John's family moved out the next day.

Which family do you think was not using common sense? How do you know? Or were they both using different common sense—that is sense that was common to a different reference group?

Why was their friendship enough to sustain them at first, but not over the long term?

Reflect on your own family. What kinds of differences or conflicts have you had come up with other families around the following areas:

Meals

Holidays and gift giving

Clothing

Hygiene

Work and personal responsibility

Ownership of personal items

Conversation / Background Noise

Time (as in what is considered on-time)

WHAT DO YOU THINK?

The differences in this activity were between families from the same basic ethnic and socioeconomic background. Have you seen cultural differences between families that are otherwise similar?

If differences and misunderstandings like this are possible between culturally similar people, how much misunderstanding do you think might be possible between culturally different people?

How might the awareness of different kinds of "common sense" help you understand those who are different from you?

SUMMARY

SEEING CULTURE | 2

Invisible things are hard to see.

As discussed in **Unit 1**, culture is more of a process than a "thing", and it can be understood as "how people do their stuff together". The patterns that come together around how we answer the questions of life are often difficult to see, especially because when we grow up in a culture, everything is so normal to us that we do not even realize that we are in that culture! It is kind of like this question: **What's the last thing a fish discovers?**

Marshall McLuhan suggested that the answer is "water." Actually what he said was:

> "One thing about which fish know exactly nothing is water, since they have no anti-environment which would enable them to perceive the element they live in."
>
> - *McCluhan, M. & Fiore, Q. (1968). War and Peace in the Global Village. (P. 175). New York: McGraw-Hill*

This unit suggests ways that you can practice seeing the 'cultural water' that you live in. According to McLuhan's idea, one of the ways that we can do that is by coming into contact with contrasting cultural systems (what he refers to as anti-environments).

What that means for you:

This Unit includes examples from a lot of different cultures. Depending on what cultural setting you are planning to work in, you may find yourself wondering why you need to learn about people in Africa, Asia, Europe, or Latin America. These different cultures are presented as examples of **other ways of doing things**. At this stage, the point is not really to learn about them as much as it is to learn about your own culture!

Topic Three starts with a kind of culture difference that may be easier to see – socioeconomic difference.

Topic Four presents another set of differences that may be familiar to you around intercultural conflict styles.

Topic Five introduces many different frameworks that you can use as hypotheses when interacting with people from other cultures.

Topic Six looks briefly into the role that language plays in shaping the way that people from different groups think.

WHAT DO YOU THINK?

Have you spent much time in a culture other than your own? If so, did you learn anything about your own culture through that experience?

What do you think you can learn about your culture by studying other cultures?

TOPIC THREE: SOCIOECONOMIC CULTURE

BIG IDEA #9: POVERTY, MIDDLE CLASS, AND WEALTH ALL HAVE THEIR OWN CULTURES

Depending on which social class you come from, this may already be obvious to you, but poverty, middle class, and wealth each has its own culture. People in poverty and wealth tend to be more aware of this phenomenon, but if you're from the middle class this may be harder to see. The reason is that middle class, in America, is considered "normal." TV shows, magazines, pop fiction, and even advertising all tend to focus on the middle class demographic. So, if you're middle class that may mean that you have never really encountered a significant contrast (anti-environment) to your middle class lifestyle, values, and patterns.

People in poverty and wealth may be somewhat more aware of their cultural patterns, or at least that they are not part of the middle class. If you find that most advertisements on the TV don't relate to you, you very well might not be in the middle class.

ACTIVITY 2.1 | SOCIOECONOMIC CLASS CULTURE IN ADVERTISING

Advertisement 1:

It's summer, with rich green trees and a neatly kept lawn that has been mowed with straight lines, maybe even professionally. In the background birds are singing, but no other noises common to the city (sirens, cars, people talking, music, etc). Two white kids – a boy with freckles and a girl with braided pigtails – kick a soccer ball in the background. A slim white woman wearing bright colors crouches in front of a new-looking washer and dryer in a fairly new house with painted wood trim, bright lighting, and plenty of room. She explains how happy she is that her new laundry detergent does such a good job of getting the grass stains out of the children's clothes. From the look on her face, you might get the impression that this is one of the most important moments of the week.

Who is the laundry advertisement targeted toward? How do you know?

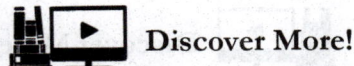 **Discover More!**

Follow these links for examples of similar videos:

Advertisement 2:

A celebrity (who is less famous now than he used to be) stands on the right third of the screen, with a nondescript empty room behind him. The primary color comes from the celebrity himself, dressed to the nines. A green and white frame at the bottom of the screen lists the name of a company that has "money" in the title. The celebrity talks directly to you, promising a quick and easy payday of $1000 for a big bill, car repair, or some kind of emergency. You only have to make $750 a month and be 18 years old. They won't even do a credit check! The celebrity fades off the screen, and a friendly but authoritative white man's voice reinforces the message – you can have $1000 by tomorrow! Twelve lines of disclaimer text are crammed into about a third of the screen.

Who is the payday loan advertisement targeted toward? How do you know?

 **Discover More!**

Follow these links for examples of similar videos:

Advertisement 3:

The clip opens with three symbols of power and strength: a giant wave, a tornado, and a mountain. A smartly dressed young black girl is the narrator, and she tells a tale about giants that roam around unchecked. After a lengthy setup, during which there are images of working-class Americans doing various kinds of labor the girl says "We walk out of the shadows, quietly walk out of the dark, and strike." Immediately, you hear a luxury sports car rev its engine and watch about 10 seconds of a single thrilling speeding car. The scene fades to black and silent text proclaims that this company is the opposite of ordinary.

Who is this advertisement targeted toward? How do you know?

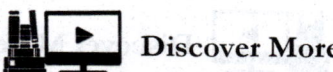 **Discover More!**

Follow this link for an examples of a similar video:

The differences between socioeconomic classes are more significant than just how much disposable money is available. There are more significant underlying themes that develop as people in each class answer the basic questions of life. What sells to one group of people may be completely un-relatable to another group because of differences in values and circumstances that don't apply across groups.

What values might each of the three advertisements have been trying to appeal to?

As we move forward into this exploration of class culture, remember that culture is how people do their stuff together. That means we can use the idea of culture as a way to understand the patterns of people in poverty, the middle class, and wealth.

 **Discover More!**

The following activity is adapted from Ruby Payne's book *A Framework for Understanding Poverty,* which covers these ideas thoroughly. Follow the link for more information on the book!

 ACTIVITY 2.2 | SPECIALIZED SKILLS

Place a check next to each of the items below that you think of as being a normal skill or activity for you or for the people that you are *most* comfortable associating with. If you do not know what one of the items means, skip it:

Set One:
- ☐ Read a menu in French, English, and another language.
- ☐ Have several favorite restaurants in different countries of the world.
- ☐ Know how to hire a decorator to identify appropriate themes and acquire exclusive décor items.
- ☐ Know who my preferred financial advisor, legal service, designer, and domestic-employment service are.
- ☐ Have at least two personal residences that are staffed and maintained year-round.
- ☐ Know how to ensure confidentiality and loyalty from my domestic staff.
- ☐ Have at least two or three "screens" that keep people whom I do not wish to see away from me.
- ☐ Fly in my own plane or the company plane.
- ☐ Know how to enroll my children in the preferred private schools.
- ☐ Know how to host the parties that "key" people attend.
- ☐ Serve on the boards of at least two charities.

❑ Can access the Junior League, the Press Club, and exclusive country-clubs at my leisure.

❑ Support or buy the work of a particular artist.

❑ Know how to read corporate financial statements, make decisions in the stock market, and analyze my own financial statements or have dedicated personnel to do this for me.

Add up the number of checks you made: _____ out of 14.

Set Two:

❑ Know which churches and sections of town have the best rummage sales.

❑ Know which thrift stores have "bag sales" and when.

❑ Know which grocery stores' and restaurants' garbage bins can be accessed for thrown-away food.

❑ Know how to get someone out of jail.

❑ Know how to physically fight and defend myself physically.

❑ Know how to get a gun, even if I have a police record.

❑ Know how to keep my clothes from being stolen at the Laundromat.

❑ Know what problems to look for in a used car.

❑ Know how to live without a bank account (including savings, checking, and credit cards).

❑ Know how to live without electricity and how to get minutes for a pay-as-you-go phone.

❑ Know how to use a knife as scissors.

❑ Able to entertain a group of friends with my personality and my stories.

❑ Know what to do when I don't have money to pay the bills.

❑ Know how to move out of my house or apartment in half a day.

❑ Know how to get and use food stamps or an electronic card for benefits.

❑ Know where the free medical clinics are.

❑ Very good at trading and bartering.

❑ I can get by without a car.

Add up the number of checks you made: _____ out of 18.

Set Three:

❑ I know how to get my children into Little League, piano lessons, soccer, etc.

❑ I know how to properly set a table.

❑ My children know the best name brands in clothing.

- ❏ I know how to order in a nice restaurant.
- ❏ I know how to use a credit card, checking account, and savings account — and I understand how to maximize the employer contribution on my 401K or 403B.
- ❏ I understand term life insurance, disability insurance, and 20/ 80 medical insurance policy, as well as homeowner's insurance, flood insurance, and replacement insurance.
- ❏ I talk to my children about going to college and have a 529 for their college expenses.
- ❏ I know how to get one of the best interest rates on my new-car loan.
- ❏ I understand the difference among the principal, interest, PMI and escrow statements on my house payment.
- ❏ I know how to help my children with their homework and do not hesitate to call the school if I need additional information.
- ❏ I know how to decorate the house for the different holidays.
- ❏ I know how to get a library card.
- ❏ I know how to use most of the tools in the garage.
- ❏ I repair items in my house almost immediately when they break — or know a repair service and call it.

Add up the number of checks you made: _____ out of 14.

Circle the number of checks you made in each column:

Set One	Set Two	Set Three
14	18	14
13	16–17	13
12	14–15	12
11	12–13	11
10	10–11	10
9	9	9
8	8	8
7	7	7
6	6	6
5	5	5
4	4	4
3	3	3
2	2	2
1	1	1
0	0	0

Which set was most familiar to you? List a few real-life examples:

In the sets that you identified less with, what items were confusing or completely unfamiliar?

Select an item that you identified with, and write an explanation targeted to someone from one of the other from one of the other groups (What does it mean, and why is it important).

What about life for the people in your group (patterns, friends, relatives, etc) reinforces the need to be skilled at the items you are skilled at? Explain your answer.

What about your life (your own patterns, your friends, your relatives, etc.) makes it possible for you to not be skilled at the items that you are not skilled at? Explain your answer.

Having identified primarily with one of the groups, what would it take for you to gain the skills of the other groups?

Objection? If you found that you had a high rating that was roughly the same in more than one group, this can be understood as a function of being bi-cultural. As described in Big Idea #2, you have multiple levels of culture, so it is entirely possible that you could identify with certain skills of both poverty and the middle class, or of middle class and wealth. It is rather less common, but certainly not impossible, to have skills of both poverty and wealth.

Big Idea#10: Cultural patterns make sense

As you may have realized, the groups of skills listed above are ordered as follows: Wealth, Poverty, and Middle Class. Each of the skills familiar to a particular socioeconomic group make sense within that group.

As discussed in **Unit One**, culture involves the following process:

The first step, How We Do Life, is in reaction to some need or opportunity faced by the group. In every case the group must choose how to **adapt** to the situation. Some of the responses are in the long-term best interest of the group – these are called **adaptive** responses. Other responses create a threat to the group in the long run – these are called **maladaptive** responses.

Whether a group's responses are adaptive or maladaptive, one of the important things to consider is that the resultant patterns make sense to the group.

**Decision:
How we do life**

Supporting Beliefs

**Becomes Common
Sense**

For example, consider the following cultural group:

ACTIVITY 2.3 | CULTURAL ADAPTATION IN PRACTICE

> **Body Ritual among the Nacirema**
> *by Horace Mitchell Miner*
>
> *The modern anthropologist has become so familiar with the diverse ways in which different people behave in similar situations he is rarely surprised by even the strangest customs. Nevertheless, the magical beliefs and practices of the Nacirema are so unusually strange that it seems useful to describe them as an example of the extremes of human behavior.*
>
> *Professor Linton first introduced the Nacirema to anthropologists twenty years ago, but the culture of this people is still very poorly understood. They are group living in the territory between the Cree people, the Yaqui and Tarahumare. Little is known of their origin, although tradition states that they came from the east. According to Nacirema myth, their nation was originated by a culture hero, Notgnihsaw a great warrior with wooden teeth.*

Nacirema culture is devoted to economic pursuits and ritual activity. The focus of this activity is the human body, the appearance and health of which are major concerns for the people. Many of the Nacirema's traditions are based on preserving bodily health and youth.

The basic belief of the culture is that the human body is ugly and that it naturally becomes weak and filled with disease. However it is believed that people can avoid these evils by using magic and rituals. Every household has one or more shrines devoted to such rituals. Very powerful individuals in the society have several shrines in their houses and, in fact, houses are said to be better if they have more shrines. Most houses are constructed from wood and plaster, but shrine rooms are walled with expensive stone.

Shrine rituals are not family ceremonies, they are private and secret. Rituals are normally only discussed with children, they are too personal to be discussed with other adults.

The main focus of the shrine is a box or chest which is built into the wall. Many charms and magical potions are kept in this chest and the natives believe that without these things they would not be able to live. The charms and potions are received mainly through powerful medicine men. As such, medicine men are very highly regarded in Nacireman society. After receiving such potion, medicine men must be rewarded with gifts of great value. Medicine men practice their craft in a latipso.

Upon entering the latipso, Naciremans are required to strip naked. Those who do not respond favorably to the potions of the medicine men often undergo a latipso temple ceremony. These ceremonies can be so harsh on a person's body that those who enter the latipso never recover, sometime the ceremony ends up killing them. If the ceremony is successful, Naciremans are not allowed to leave the temple until they provide a gift of great value.

Beneath the charm-box is a small bowl. Each day every member of the family enters the shrine room, bows his head before the charm-box, and goes through a religious cleansing ceremony. The holy waters are received from the Water Temple of the community.

Another daily body ritual performed by everyone includes a mouth-rite. This ritual involves a practice which may seem horrible. It was reported to me that the ritual consists of inserting a small bundle of hog hairs into the mouth, with certain magical ointments, and then moving the bundle in a series of gestures.

Approximately twice a year the Nacirema will journey to the holy mouth man. There they will voluntarily undergo a ritual whereby the holy mouth may jab and stick the person with a number of sharp instruments often causing great pain and blood. Such traditions show that the Nacirema value and even enjoy bodily pain. This theory is supported by another Nacirema tradition involving scraping and cutting the surface of the skin. Similar to the medicine man, the holy mouth man is part of Nacireman society's upper class.

Our review of the ritual life of the Nacirema has certainly shown them to be a people who believe a great deal in magic and it is hard to understand how they have managed to survive so long.

– Miner, H.M., "Body Ritual Among the Nacirema", *American Anthropologist*, vol 58: pp. 503–507, June 1956.

What kind of adaptations have the Nacirema made?

Can you see the basic pattern of 1. Decision about how to live, 2. Beliefs to support patterns, 3. Patterns become common sense? Give an example.

Do you think that Nacireman practices make sense to the Nacirema?

Reverse the order of the letters of the following words, and then reread the article Nacirema, Latipso(h), Notgnihsaw.

What difference does this make in your understanding of the article?

The basic aim of the previous activity is to see that cultural patterns make sense to the cultural insider, no matter how bizarre they may seem to a cultural outsider. Returning to the idea of culture in economic classes, consider Ruby Payne's explanation of hidden rules:

Hidden rules: the unspoken cues and habits of a group. All groups have hidden rules; you know you belong when you don't have to explain anything you say or do. These rules are held by racial, ethnic, religious, regional, and cultural groups… to name a few. An individual's cultural fabric is made up of many threads, one of which is economic class.

. . . The hidden rules arise from the environment in which a person lives, that they help persons survive in the class in which they were raised. This means that the rules of class are not to be criticized, but that we simply add options, new rules, a wider range of responses, an ability to negotiate more environments.

Ruby Payne (2005) *A Framework for Understanding Poverty*

WHAT DO YOU THINK?

Ruby Payne argues that the hidden rules of culture help people to survive, but we know that maladaptive hidden rules actually hurt or inhibit people as they try to advance. Why should we, according to Payne, not criticize these hidden rules?

Payne seems to argue that it is important that we understand that cultural practices make sense in their own context, even if outsiders don't understand them. Can you think of cultural practices that make sense in your culture that outsiders don't understand?

What does Payne suggest as an alternative to criticizing the hidden rules of peoples' class cultures?

Big Idea #11: To an extent, we are all trying to accomplish the same things

Despite the major differences that can be found between cultures, there are certain similarities that all people experience in some way or another. Payne explores this idea through the lens of socioecononmic status. If you have not already done so, consider reading and reflecting on *A Framework for Understanding Poverty* by Ruby Payne (2005), especially chapters 3 & 4. Use the following questions to guide you.

What human goals does Payne imply are common to all people?

In what way do those goals play out differently depending on socioeconomic status affiliation?

What goals might you have assumed were common to all people that Payne suggested were unique to your socioeconomic status affiliation?

TOPIC FOUR: FINDING CULTURE *EVERYWHERE*

Culture affects nearly everything about how we as people interpret the world around us. Although it is true (and importantly true!) that all people share certain core attributes, it is also true that our cultures shape the ways in which we interpret even those core attributes. For example, even though it is true that everyone needs to eat, this does not mean that food holds the same meaning or is experienced in the same ways across different cultural groups.

Looking for culture. Cultures abound. Think about what this means in your context. Here are a couple of examples:

If you are a college student then you might on a weekly basis, interact with culture in the following settings:

- Your particular major
- Your area of focus within that major may have yet another cultural subset
- Classes you have with profs that teach in other academic disciplines may have noticeably different cultural elements
- The diverse groups that are present at your college (which are numerous – socioeconomic, ethnic, national, linguistic, vocational, extra-curricular activities, etc)
- The culture of the college's location (i.e. rural, small town, urban)
- The state and nation in which the college is located
- Your local church setting
- Your place of employment
- Members of your family

By contrast, if you are a worker at a non-profit youth organization in the Midwest you might experience the following cultural settings:

- The youth you work with: especially Generational Culture (i.e., youth, young adult, adult, elder)
- The youths' families: especially Ethnic/Racial and Socioeconomic
- Your ministry's culture: including departmental culture, Christian culture, Board culture
- "The System": especially bureaucratic culture, expert culture, social worker culture, judicial, courts, prison, probation
- Church culture: especially denominational, sometimes ethnic/racial and socioeconomic
- Yourself: your own complex blend of cultural identities
- Your city's culture: the specific blend of assumptions and patterns necessary for success in the city
- Great Plains / Midwest culture: regional culture
- US culture: patterns of national culture, especially including dominant cultural patterns and assumptions

WHAT DO YOU THINK?

Think through your week. What kinds of culture did you navigate through this week? Give examples.

Which cultures do people that you work with need to be able to navigate? For example, if you are becoming a teacher, what cultures do your students need to be able to navigate? If you are moving into social work, which cultural groups do your clients need to be able to navigate? Explain.

How might you be able to coach those people that you identified in the previous question see culture at play in these different settings?

TOPIC FIVE: CULTURE GENERAL FRAMEWORKS

Having looked at cultural patterns in socioeconomic classes, we now turn to **frameworks** that we can use to understand patterns across cultures. Remember, the goal of this Unit is **Seeing Culture**. This topic is designed to provide only an elementary understanding of key frameworks that you are likely to encounter. There are more than 25 common frameworks that can be used to understand cultural values, patterns, and behaviors. Although you may eventually want to become familiar with all of those, the goal here is to practice recognizing how culture shapes the way in which people (especially groups of people) interact with the world and with each other.

HOW TO USE THESE FRAMEWORKS

Each of these frameworks uses the idea of a **continuum**. Each continuum usually has one key idea, with two major approaches to how people interact with that idea. If you recall the idea of generalizations from Big Idea #3, people from any given culture will tend toward certain expressions of those ideas, while people from another culture may tend toward other expressions of the same ideas.

Remember that any given culture will have a distribution of tendencies like the one demonstrated below. So, although it may be possible to say that a culture tends toward Approach One or Approach Two (or somewhere in between), we do expect to find individual members of the culture that are outside of that normal pattern.

BIG IDEA #12: INDIVIDUALISM AND COLLECTIVISM ARE TWO WAYS TO EXPERIENCE IDENTITY

One of the most important frameworks that we will use is **individualism – collectivism**. You have probably heard of this framework before, although the way that this framework is used in popular culture can be misleading. Individualism – collectivism, for example is not a political or economic ideal.

Instead, this continuum relates primarily to how people within a culture define the *self*. People on the individualist side of the spectrum identify primarily as an individual, and only secondarily as a member of a group. On the other hand, people on the collectivist side of the spectrum identify primarily as a member of a group, and only secondarily as an individual.

This distinction has significant consequences, but it is helpful not to conflate this topic with other related ideas. For example, although it may make sense to connect the framework called "relationship orientation" with collectivist cultures, those are actually two different frameworks, and you will ultimately find these more useful if you keep them separate.

ACTIVITY 2.4 | IDENTIFYING INDIVIDUALIST AND COLLECTIVIST PATTERNS

Circle the letter I or C to indicate whether the statement is *more* individualistic or collectivistic.

I C	My goal in life is to make a name for myself.	
I C	My goal in life is to make my family proud.	
I C	I am afraid that if I make a mistake it will reflect badly on my people.	
I C	I am afraid that if I make a mistake it will hurt my image.	
I C	When I meet people, I always want to know what they do.	
I C	When meeting people, it is important to know their family name.	
I C	I dress to show my style.	
I C	I dress to show my affiliation.	
I C	When people look at me, I want them to see me for me.	
I C	It is better not to be noticed – the nail that sticks up is the one that gets hammered down.	

I C	If I go to college, I'm going to pick the school that I like best.
I C	If I go to college, my family will select the school for me.
I C	My dream job is one where I am really satisfied.
I C	My dream job is one that makes my family proud.
I C	My parents will choose my vocation.
I C	When I mess up, I am mostly upset because I know that the consequences can affect my future opportunities.
I C	When I mess up, I am mostly upset because I am afraid that my family might disown me.
I C	I am really proud of my family's name.
I C	I am really proud of what I have accomplished.

It is important to recognize that this list is by no means comprehensive, so do not use it as an assessment. Instead, use it as a way to understand patterns of thought and value. At the same time, remember that even a culture that identifies with the general pattern of individualism or collectivism may not identify with any of the particular items above. Culture is dynamic and fluid, and it is important not to assume that you know more about a person's experience of being part of their culture than you actually do.

WHAT DO YOU THINK?

What thoughts do you have about individualism and collectivism? Do you have a preference for one over the other?

Majority American culture tends toward individualism. If you are individualistic and are working with a student, client, or coworker who is collectivist, what kinds of misunderstandings might you experience?

ACTIVITY 2.5 | UNDERSTANDING EFFECTS

Consider the following example:

One of Phil's clients has the opportunity to advance his education through a scholarship to a local university in a field he is interested in. Phil is thrilled with the opportunity and goes out of his way to help the client get the scholarship by writing a letter of recommendation, recruiting other letters of recommendation, and walking his client through the application process.

After months of waiting, Phil finds out that the scholarship selection committee chose his client to receive a full-ride scholarship. For some reason, though, the client does not seem as excited about the opportunity as Phil expected. As the semester in which he is to start college classes nears, the client is increasingly evasive and distant. Phil assumes that the client must be afraid to start classes as a first generation college student, but when he tries to line up support services the client does not follow up on any appointments.

Finally, the semester starts and the client does not show up for the first week of classes.

Why do you think Phil's client is not taking advantage of this opportunity to advance his education?

At this point what are you thinking about Phil's client?

There are, of course, many possible explanations. Consider this example of how individualism / collectivism might contribute to this situation:

Phil finally gets the opportunity to confront the client about squandering this opportunity to advance his education. This charge upsets him, but he doesn't disagree with Phil, who finally asks in agitation "Don't you see! This is your big chance to get ahead. You can really make something of yourself and escape the problems of your neighborhood! You can really be successful!" The client, although disturbed by these words is ultimately unmoved by them. He finally responds "Don't you see – that kind of success is failure in the eyes of my family. If I go to college and do well, I might become a big man. But that is not success. If I get a good job and have to move far from here and I neglect my grandmother, I am a failure. It is too much to ask."

How was Phil's attempt to motivate the client coming from individualistic values?

Why didn't this connect with the client?

Can you imagine another way to motivate the client that might resonate with his collectivistic values?

AT THE INTERSECTION

Joel walked into his house and saw his roommate Benjamin, sitting on the couch with a frown on his face. Benjamin explained to Joel that he had just gotten had an argument with his mother over the phone. Benjamin was an education major and wanted to switch majors but his mother was adamantly opposed to his decision. Joel told Benjamin that this was not a big deal as he was an adult and did not need to follow his parent's advice. Benjamin tried to explain to Joel that it was considered a disgrace in his culture to go against his parent's wishes. Joel insisted that this was a small issue and that Benjamin's parents would just have to get over it somehow. Joel left the room feeling content that he had been able to help Benjamin with his problem. Meanwhile, Benjamin slumped low into the couch, frustrated that Joel did not understand how important it was to him that his mother gave her permission for him to switch majors.

BIG IDEA #13: TASK AND RELATIONSHIP

PRODUCTIVE FOCUS

TASK ⟵⟶ RELATIONSHIP

This big idea may be familiar to you, and it is fairly self-explanatory, so we will not dwell here too long. One important feature to recognize is that even very relationally oriented majority culture Americans still tend to be far more **task oriented** than people in cultures that have a dominant tendency toward a **relational orientation**. I have also sometimes had students confuse their own laziness with a relational orientation. These two patterns, although they may appear related, are actually quite different.

True relational orientation requires a tremendous amount of work in the social sphere. It is not an exchange of work for relationship, but rather an **exchange of task-based work for relational-based work.** Relational cultures have highly sophisticated tools and protocols for building and maintaining relationships, just as task-based cultures have highly sophisticated tools and protocols for accomplishing tasks. A friend of mine from West Africa jokes that in America, time is money, while in Africa relationship is money.

ACTIVITY 2.6 | JIM IN KIBERA

Jim had big plans. He worked very hard to bring about a partnership between his largely white American church and a community development ministry in Kenya. After a hard fought victory in the missions committee of his church, he finally secured the funding to go to Kenya for a week to set up the project. He arrived in Kenya and received a tour of the Kibera slum from a local pastor and learned about the tremendous need in that area. On his second day in Kenya, moved with compassion, Jim emailed the church and told them that there was definitely a partnership in Kenya. The missions committee wrote back affirming the partnership and mentioned that they had made contact with a solar panel manufacturer. At the end of the week Jim met with the pastor to tell him that his Church was ready to commit, and that they could begin installing solar panels in the upcoming summer. In the meeting the pastor appeared confused, and communicated that the people in Kibera have many pressing needs.

Kibera: Kenya. By Valter Campanato/Abr CC 2007

Jim responded "of course, but we have to get our foot in the door! Once we get started, then we can begin to learn about what's really needed in Kibera and how we can fix it!" He returned to the US and began fundraising for the major solar panel project.

In what ways did Jim's task orientation play out?

What might the pastor have been communicating (indirectly) when he said that there were many pressing needs for the people in Kibera?

Overall, how effective do you expect Jim's involvement in Kenya will be?

Do you tend to emphasize task or relationship for your productive focus?

How would you help a relationally oriented person succeed in a task-oriented society?

BIG IDEA# 14: POLYCHRONIC AND MONOCHRONIC

When interacting with different cultures, competing views of time often cause some of the most obvious disconnects. There are two major ways that people view time: **polychronic** and **monochronic**. Some cultures view time as limited and linear, while others view it as cyclical and abundant.

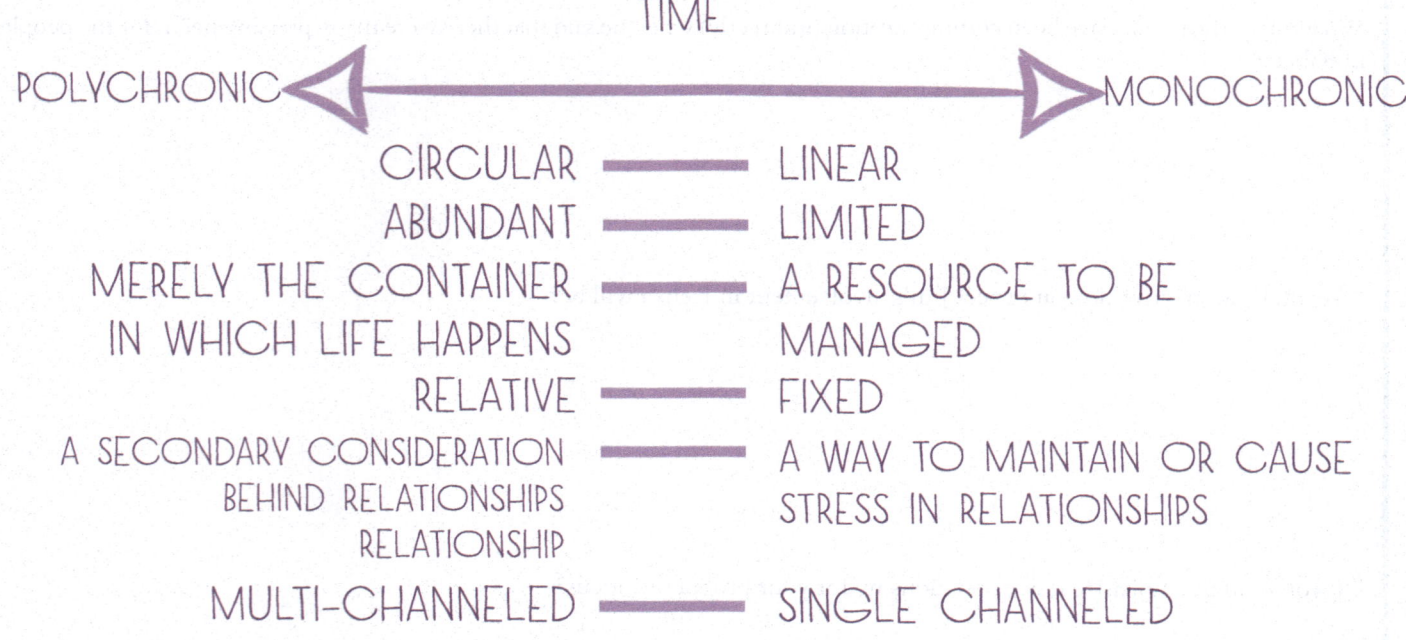

TIME

POLYCHRONIC ← → MONOCHRONIC

CIRCULAR	LINEAR
ABUNDANT	LIMITED
MERELY THE CONTAINER IN WHICH LIFE HAPPENS	A RESOURCE TO BE MANAGED
RELATIVE	FIXED
A SECONDARY CONSIDERATION BEHIND RELATIONSHIPS RELATIONSHIP	A WAY TO MAINTAIN OR CAUSE STRESS IN RELATIONSHIPS
MULTI-CHANNELED	SINGLE CHANNELED

AT THE INTERSECTION

Raquel and Kelly worked at the same summer camp. During training, they were paired up and put in charge of teaching a dancing class. On the first day, Kelly picked the song and played it off her phone for the class to listen. While the song was playing, Kelly's phone rang and she paused the song to take the call. Over the phone came a very loud and excited voice, talking really fast. Raquel frowned at this, as camp rules stated that camp counselors were discouraged from using their phones for personal reasons. Still, she rationalized that this could be an important call. As moments passed, she realized that this was not an important call after all. She threw a look at Kelly, hoping Kelly would catch on that this was against camp regulations. Kelly looked up and saw Raquel's face. She began explaining to her friend that she was busy at a camp, but her friend continued talking. This went on for five minutes and Raquel had enough. She signaled to Kelly, demanding that Kelly end the call immediately. Kelly finally hung up and apologized to Raquel, but Raquel would not hear any of Kelly's excuses. Why did Kelly take the call if she knew that it was not urgent? In her mind, Raquel decided that Kelly was an irresponsible person and did not care about the class because she was more concerned about talking on the phone when she could have rejected the call in the first place.

Here are some common **misperceptions**:

Monochronic people tend to perceive polychronic people as:

lazy, always late, rude, self-centered, undisciplined.

Polychronic people tend to perceive monochronic people as:

hyper, insensitive, rude, self-centered, too serious (generally about the wrong things).

People using polychronic and monochronic perspectives can also experience difficulties in interaction due to varied perceptions of timelines for projects. For example, because people who use a monochromic perspective tend to view time as limited, there is often a significant **sense of urgency**, whether that be the timeline within a day's activities, or the timeline for a major project that will last several months. On the other hand, people who use the polychromic perspective tend to be aware of many other "time-related" issues, such as **social and climatic seasons** and **relational timelines**, both of which may be more difficult for those who use the monochromic perspective to see. Because the polychronic perspective sees time as the container in which life happens, rather than as a resource spent to make life happen, **time-based urgency is not significantly motivating**, which stands in stark contrast to monochronic people, who are regularly evaluating and **reprioritizing the time-sensitive urgency of different tasks**.

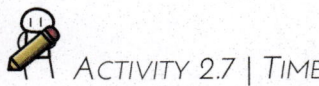

ACTIVITY 2.7 | TIME

A woman who has recently moved to the US has sought out ½ day child care assistance for her two young boys so she can work. She drops them off at the daycare at five in the morning and is told that she needs to pick them up at ten o'clock. She seems surprised and suggests that she will be earlier than that. Yet ten o'clock comes and goes and there is no sign of her. By noon there is still no sign of her, and the daycare manager, who cannot reach the mother by phone, calls Child Protective Services according to the daycare's policy. Finally, at three o'clock in the afternoon the mother arrives to pick up her children. She is mortified when she is told that she has to meet with a case worker to discuss the abandonment of her children.

What scenarios could explain the mother's behavior? Try to think of at least two.

There are at least five main scenarios than can explain the mother's behavior.

1. She might not have understood the instructions to pick her children up at ten o'clock due to a language barrier.

2. She might have thought that the pickup time was ten o'clock PM.

3. She might have understood the pickup time was ten AM, but run into some kind of trouble that kept her late.

4. She might have understood that the pickup time was ten AM, but be from a polychronic culture in which such times are simply considered reference, rather than specific.

5. She might have been from a culture that uses a sun-based clock, where sunup is one o'clock. In such a case, she would have thought that the pickup time was more like four o'clock in the afternoon! In that case she actually might have thought she was early!

Any of these cases is possible. It is safe to assume that due to her shocked reaction, for some reason or another she did not think she was late. The daycare, on the other hand, would have been understandably frustrated from a monochronic point of view.

How might you explain this situation to the daycare?

To Child Protective Services (which had been called according to the daycare's policy)?

To the mother?

AT THE INTERSECTION

Janna was on her college's Student Government. She was excited to work with the student executive team as the Secretary of Student Senate. On the first meeting, Janna walked into the meeting hall and sat down. After setting her things down, she looked up and saw that people were staring at her. This seemed weird to her, but she decided to shake it off. She took out her laptop and pulled out a word program to take down notes. As she started typing, she realized that the discussion was already on the second point on the agenda. She was puzzled as she could not have been later than five minutes. After the meeting, Curtis, the president of Student Government approached her and reprimanded her for being late. He commented on how her actions were irresponsible and disrespectful. He also told her that she was setting a bad example for the rest of the team. He let her go with a warning that he would take disciplinary action against her if she continued wasting other people's time by showing up late. Janna was surprised that Curtis had taken up such a firm tone with her, especially since they were good friends. She did not understand how being five minutes late was the same as being disrespectful.

BIG IDEA #15: CRISIS AND NON CRISIS

PLANNING

CRISIS ⟵———————⟶ NON-CRISIS

The **crisis / non-crisis orientation** is related closely to polychronic / monochronic perspectives but offers a distinct lens through which to view the way people interact. As with most cultural patterns, misperceptions around crisis / non-crisis orientation tend to lead to judgments about the character of the "other" person. Let's look at an example before clarifying the definition of the crisis and non-crisis orientations:

ACTIVITY 2.8 | LIVING FOR THE CRISIS OR THE MOMENT?

This brief story illustrates one of the principle differences between crisis orientation and non-crisis orientation. Crisis orientation, represented by the narrator, looks ahead for what crises might happen and seeks ways to **mitigate** (or reduce) the bad effects of the crises in advance. In the preceding story *circle the crises* that the narrator perceives which do not seem to be perceived in the same ways by his hosts.

It is a warm afternoon in West Africa. We are sitting under a mango tree, enjoying tea, which can take about 3 hours, and moving back and forth between business and relational conversation. An hour into the tea time, we see a large bank of clouds approaching, and a couple of the elder men make comments about it, noting that it will probably rain. We continue to sit under the tree as the wind picks up, blowing red dust into everything. I wonder what kind of bacteria have just blown into my mouth and nose riding on the dust. I'm already hoping that using shared tea cups will not get me sick with typhoid. I begin to get uncomfortable because we should have moved inside by now. Instead of moving inside, the tea maker begins the next round of tea – a process that takes a minimum of 15 minutes. The clouds get closer, and we can begin to smell the rain in the air. Another gust of wind, and I am beyond ready to go inside. We continue talking, with me apparently the only one who is uncomfortable about the weather. Finally, it starts to rain – just little sprinkles at first, so the mango tree protects us. We continue sitting under the tree. Then, suddenly, the men spring into action. Within a minute, we and our tea stove are inside, just as it begins to pour one of the hardest rains I've seen in years. We escape the brunt of it and are just a little bit wet, and continue to enjoy the good conversation over tea.

What are the benefits and limitations of a crisis orientation?

Examples of benefits: contingency plans in place ahead of disasters; ready to mobilize when crises inevitably occur; development of best practices can limit harm and maximize helpfulness of interventions.

What are the benefits and limitations of a non-crisis orientation?

Examples of benefits: more awareness of life in the present moment; does not waste time and energy preparing for crises that do not end up happening; able to access "folk wisdom" from non-experts.

Lingenfelter and Mayers (2003, p. 71) present the following comparison of the crisis and non-crises orientations.

CRISIS ORIENTATION	NON-CRISIS ORIENTATION
ANTICIPATE CRISIS	DOWNPLAY POSSIBILITY OF CRISIS
EMPHASIZE PLANNING	FOCUS ON ACTUAL EXPERIENCE
SEEKS QUICK RESOLUTION TO AVOID AMBIGUITY	AVOIDS TAKING ACTION; DELAYS DECISIONS
REPEATEDLY FOLLOWS A SINGLE AUTHORITATIVE, PREPLANNED PROCEDURE	SEEKS AD HOC SOLUTIONS FROM MULTIPLE AVAILABLE OPTIONS
SEEKS EXPERT ADVICE	DISTRUSTS EXPERTS

ACTIVITY 2.9 | SEEING CRISES IN EVERYDAY LIFE

Create a list of elements of dominant, middle-class American life that are reflections of a crisis orientation:

examples: health insurance, tornado drills, the Red Cross, 24 hour news,

WHAT DO YOU THINK?

Consider this: For people from the crisis orientation patterns in non-crisis cultures can seem like irresponsible living. Can you think of examples of this? Why might people from the non-crisis perspective be justified in feeling that their patterns are not irresponsible?

AT THE INTERSECTION

Jason's parents had prepared him to deal with emergencies since he was a child. Safety was a priority in his family and from a young age he had memorized the number of local medical and emergency services. When Jason traveled to South Asia on a missions trip, he was shocked to discover that the dorm he was to live in for two weeks did not have an emergency plan. When he asked what to do in case of fire, he was told to run out of the building and grab the nearest hose as there were no sprinklers in the building. Jason felt that his hosts were ill-prepared to deal with emergencies and did not prioritize the safety of those living in the dormitory.

BIG IDEA #16: UNIVERSALISM AND PARTICULARISM

ETHICS

 UNIVERSALISM  PARTICULARISM

Also known as **particular** vs. **universal reference**, **universalism** and **particularism** is a very important framework to understand for interpreting ethical judgments across cultures. Universal cultures refer primarily to abstract principles, while particular cultures refer primarily to context and relationship to determine moral rightness.

The classic illustration of this idea is found in this activity, adapted from Storti (1998):

 ACTIVITY 2.10 | WHOSE SIDE ARE YOU ON?

Imagine that you are a passenger in a car driven by someone you know. You happen to notice that the speedometer reads 35 in a 25 mile-per-hour zone. Suddenly, a pedestrian appears in front of the vehicle. The driver is unable to take evasive action in time to avoid a collision, and the vehicle hits the pedestrian.

When the police are investigating the incident, will you mention what you saw on the speedometer?

What information, if any, do you feel like you need in order to be better answer this question?

In general, people who favor a universalist application of ethics will need very little if any additional information in order to answer the question. They might take into account the condition of the pedestrian, but little else. On the other hand, particularlists would tend to want information about how they knew or were related to both the driver and the pedestrian. There would likely be many other circumstantial items brought into view for the particularist.

Particularism is sometimes confused with a lack of ethical grounding, which it is not. For example, if you are a particularlist who lives in a country with a corrupt police force, and if the driver is your sister's husband (and they have three children), and if the pedestrian was not badly injured, or if the pedestrian was intoxicated, and if speed limit signs are widely disregarded anyway, then it might actually be **morally wrong** for you to do anything that would imperil the livelihood of your sister and her family. Thus, this issue is not one of whether there are ethical absolutes – it is assumed in both cases that there are ethics that govern the situation. The question is much more about *how* those ethics are applied.

Recall that cultural norms make sense in their own context. Universalist ethics tend to make more sense in a country where there is a broadly appreciated rule of law, and where the enforcement of that law is perceived to be rather just. Importantly, this perception will vary by socio-economic sub-culture.

WHAT DO YOU THINK?

Imagine this: If you had a student in your youth group who made decisions according to a particularist framework, how might s/he be perceived in a universalist American school?

How could you help a univeralist school principal understand the particularist decision making behind the student's actions?

How could you help the student understand the univeralist elements of the school system she is having trouble working with?

At The Intersection

Janet's friend Cheryl was facing a dilemma. Cheryl's mother had been involved in an accident and had fled the scene before the police arrived. Cheryl's father had taken the car to a chop shop for repair to avoid having to make an insurance report. As Cheryl shared this with Janet, she expressed the conflict she had with pretending like nothing had happened. Yet, she could not betray her own mother. Janet was alarmed that Cheryl would even consider sweeping such a big thing under the rug and urged Cheryl to do the right thing. A week later, Janet discovered that Cheryl had not taken any action and was disappointed with Cheryl for conspiring with her family to hide the hit and run.

BIG IDEA #17: MOTIVATIONS

Muller (2000) suggests that there are three primary motivations in human society. While some cultures will tend toward one or another of these, all three are to usually to some degree present in all cultures.

GUILT	Cultures on this spectrum emphasize right and wrong, good and bad, correct and incorrect. A primary cultural goal is to alleviate or avoid guilt whenever possible. Innocence (actual or supposed) is the preferred state. The ability to demonstrate innocence in oneself or others is valued. Guilt or innocence in motive can be established separately from guilt or innocence in action.	INNOCENCE
SHAME	Cultures on this spectrum emphasize honor and dishonor, which are usually located with the family, tribe, or related group, rather than just the individual. Family honor must be maintained at all costs. Those who can resolve conflict through restoring honor all around are viewed as wise. Bringing dishonor on oneself, one's family, or on others is often viewed as a moral failure.	HONOR
FEAR	Cultures on this spectrum live with a significant awareness of unseen powers and spirits. Efforts are made to appease the unseen powers, but fear of those spirits and other people dominates. Power of various kinds (economic, spiritual, physical, social, religious) is desirable and attained in whatever ways possible. Power is sometimes seen as being vested in human authority, the fear of which can be considered a valid and important trait.	POWER

ACTIVITY 2.11 | GUILT AND INNOCENCE

Dominant American culture has emphasized Guilt and Innocence over Shame and Honor or Power and Fear. This may be changing, but the power of Guilt and Innocence is still a very strong motivation for many Americans. I participated in a team development session for a group of Americans in which we presented a letter written by people that had been negatively affected by largely unintentional cultural offenses my trainees had perpetrated. The immediate desire of many of the trainees was to ask for very specific information about the offenses – who, what, when, where, why. The letter contained only two examples of the very pervasive theme of unintentional offense because the intention of those who had been offended was to present a general theme rather than to call out specific instances. Many of my trainees were unable to move forward with the steps necessary to developing the competence to avoid causing future offence without having first established whether or not they were (individually) guilty of causing offence in the first place.

How did the guilt / innocence framework shape this interaction?

The authors of the letter largely came from cultural backgrounds that emphasized shame/honor or power/fear either alongside or instead of the guilt/innocence perspective. How might this have shaped their approach to the letter?

How might the trainers have been able to better serve the interests of both the trainees and the letter writers through intentionally applying the insights of this framework?

AT THE INTERSECTION

Kaiyo's roommate Alice recently confronted her over an offense that Kaiyo had committed against her. When Kaiyo learned about her offense against Alice, she began apologizing profusely. However, Alice soon realized that Kaiyo's apology was not concerning the offense she had committed. Rather, Kaiyo apologized for the dishonor she had caused Alice to feel. Nowhere had Kaiyo acknowledged her wrong doing against Alice. Alice was confused and did not really understand what Kaiyo was apologizing for. Did Kaiyo realize that she had done something wrong? Or, was she merely apologizing to avert further conflict?

AT THE INTERSECTION

John's friend Timmy was late for their meeting. Upon arrival, Timmy apologized profusely. Timmy explained that his family had fallen upon a bout of bad fortune recently and his father had taken the entire family to seek the blessing and protection of a local shaman. At first John thought Timmy was joking, but Timmy seemed completely serious. John could not comprehend how people in the 21st century could buy into hocus pocus superstition. John thought that surely Timmy must realize that shamans are conmen and that spirits are not real!

Discover more!
Read *Honor and Shame by Roland Muller (2000)*, which also covers Guilt and Innocence, and Power and Fear (link on the left).
For additional reading, try *The Spirit Catches You and You Fall Down by Fadiman (2012) (link on the right)*.

BIG IDEA #18: SURVIVAL INTELLIGENCES

A promising area of recent research is **survival intelligences**, as conceptualized by Mark Harden (2010), a former police officer turned academic. He noticed that many attempts to engage people in urban settings were based out of a recognition of only the problems in those communities, and were focused on reducing those problems.

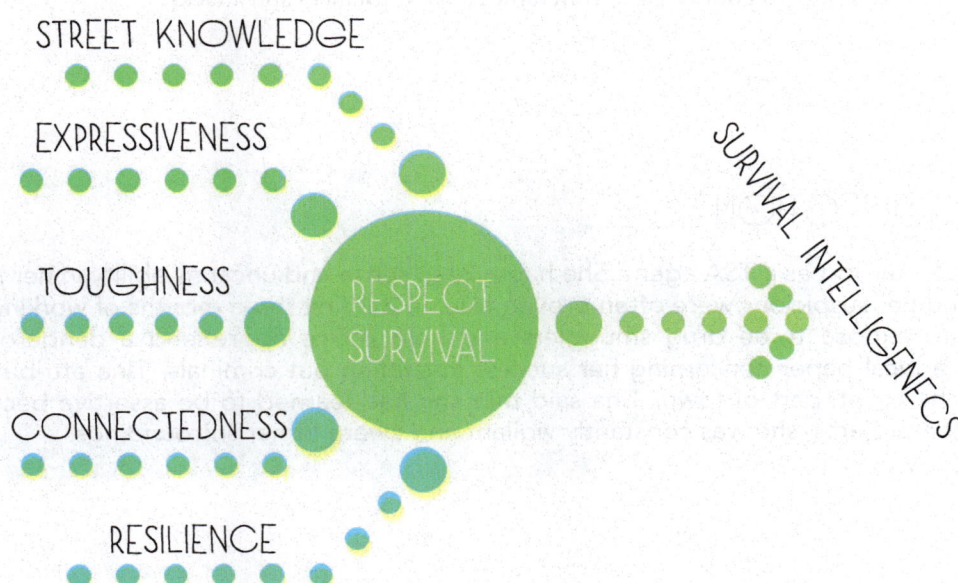

I

In particular, certain behavioral traits in inner-city urban populations were seen as being major obstacles that had to be overcome for the individuals and communities to be able to develop. Harden suggested that the common deficit-based approach sometimes used by urban and social work practitioners is not only unhelpful, but also unnecessary.

He proposed an asset-based approach, which suggests that people living in certain environments have actually developed adaptive cultural patterns. The research is still in the works, but Harden suggested that these frameworks could be understood from a cultural perspective:

In this book, we interpret these frameworks as follows.

Respect and **Survival** are two main categories, under which the following survival intelligences can be placed. For example, street knowledge can be used to gain, give, or maintain respect, but it is also necessary for survival (i.e. knowing when to avoid certain streets).

Street Knowledge knowing what to expect in a challenging urban environment, including a tacit awareness of what signals danger and safety. This involves a highly attuned and accurate situational awareness.

Expressiveness the ability to communicate in ways that are understood, whether actively (i.e. talking, fronting and other forms of acting, woofing) or passively (i.e. dress). This includes the ability to influence others through communication so as to avoid harm and maximize benefit for oneself and one's community.

Toughness a display of strength that is understood to mean both "don't mess with me" and "you don't want me to mess with you".

Connectedness refers to networks of social support, which will often provide both material and security benefits.

Resilience describes the ability to bounce back from difficult circumstances and attacks.

AT THE INTERSECTION

Tina worked at the airport as a TSA agent. She had a keen sense and uncanny ability in her job. Tina's instincts were spot on and her suspicions were often proven true. In the first three months of working for the TSA, Tina had managed to expose three drug smugglers and help police apprehend a dangerous fugitive. When interviewed by a local paper concerning her success in sniffing out criminals, Tina attributed her success to growing up in the rough part of town. Tina said that she had learned to be assertive because as a little girl growing up in the projects, she was constantly vigilant and aware of her surroundings.

WHAT DO YOU THINK?

Can you recall how you might have seen these themes play out in your own life? In the lives of others? If not, can you remember seeing these represented in media?

ACTIVITY 2.12 | APPLYING SURVIVAL INTELLIGENCE

Briefly identify how each of these Survival Intelligences would be useful (adaptive) traits in the following contexts: 1) Military / War; 2) Education; 3) Business

<u>Military/War</u>

Street knowledge

Expressiveness

Toughness

Connectedness

Resilience

Education

Street knowledge

Expressiveness

Toughness

Connectedness

Resilience

Business

Street knowledge

Expressiveness

Toughness

Connectedness

Resilience

As mentioned before, there is a tendency to treat these adaptive strategies as deficiencies rather than as assets. How can you actively work to treat these adaptations in yourself or others as assets, rather than liabilities or deficiencies?

BIG IDEA #19: ADDITIONAL FRAMEWORKS

There are, of course, many additional frameworks beyond the ones we have examined thus far. Here is a short list, again with the primary issue in the middle, and with two ends of the continuum on either side.

POWER

EQUALITY ⟵⟶ HIERARCHY

The **power** (sometimes called power distance) framework describes the ways in which some cultures appreciate a strictly regimented **hierarchy**, even to the extent that leaders may be viewed as a categorically or existentially different kind of person from non-leaders. **Egalitarian** cultures dislike reminders of power differences and prefer to view everyone as equal even if they have roles with inherent power differences. There are many variations in between these to extremes.

STATUS

ACHIEVEMENT ⟵⟶ ASCRIPTION

The way in which a person's **status** in society is determined depends on how a culture views the role of **achievement** and **ascription**. Achievement oriented cultures, sometimes called meritocracies, tend to award status based on the achievements of the individual with little or no reference to their background, family of origin, and so on. Ascription oriented cultures, on the other hand, tend to be much more interested in the facts about a person than what she or he has accomplished – family of origin and last name may be enough to set a person's social status in such a culture.

TOLERANCE OF AMBIGUITY

RISK TAKING ⟵⟶ SECURITY

Some cultures have a fairly high **tolerance for ambiguity**, which can be seen when a high value it placed on risk taking. In such a cultural context, **risk taking** is not generally considered irresponsible – instead it is valued as an important way to advance individuals and society. **Security** oriented cultures, on the other hand, tend to have a lower tolerance of ambiguity and prefer to have outcomes reasonably known in advance of attempting a new endeavor. This is not the same value as having a high value on safety/security, which may be better understood as crisis orientation. Rather, this is a sense that risks should be avoided unless there are no other legitimate options, and that even then other options should be pursued. The implications of these different approaches are particularly interesting to observe in the business and foreign policy settings.

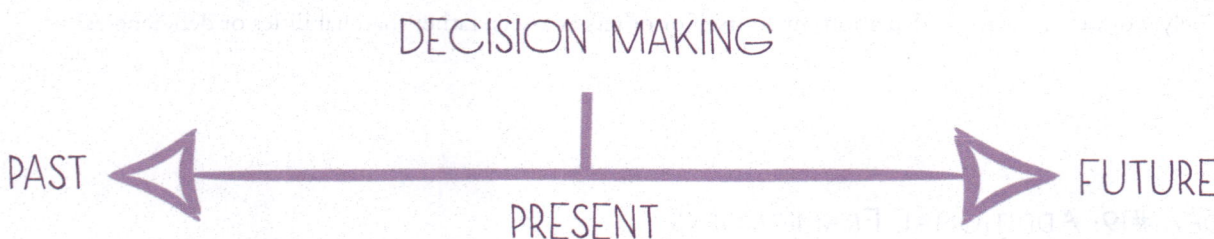

DECISION MAKING

PAST ⟵———————|———————⟶ FUTURE

PRESENT

Related to the tolerance for ambiguity, but distinct from it, is the general time orientation utilized by a culture when making decisions. Some cultures are highly tied to the **past** and view it as very relevant to **decision making**. Some are highly **future** oriented, with a concern for the long-term (i.e. 500 year) implications of decisions made today. Others are **present oriented** with a strong value on experiencing the moment now. Of course there are many other options along the continuum. My personal sense is that US American culture is near-future oriented (i.e. 5 years).

ACTIVITY

COOPERATIVE ⟵———————⟶ COMPETITIVE

The ways in which the **activities** required by individuals and groups are accomplished can vary. The main two modes are **cooperative**, where the emphasis is on collaborative participation, and **competitive**, where the emphasis is generally on comparison against another person or group (or even against one's own prior performance). Interestingly, cultures at both ends of this continuum tend to be somewhat suspicious of (or to outright dislike) activities that emphasize the other end of the continuum.

LOGIC

DEDUCTIVE ⟵———————⟶ INDUCTIVE/ ASSOCIATIVE

That there are different ways of knowing is a very important feature of culture to be aware of. At the same time, it is often very difficult to really wrap your mind around just how differently people from other cultures perceive **logic**. The **deductive/scientific** approach tends to be fairly familiar in the United States and emphasizes a linear logic, where each conclusion forms the basis of the next, which means that any idea can be divided into its component parts. Moreover, if the foundational argument is proven false, all subsequent conclusions are also considered false. On the other hand, the **inductive/associative/ intuitive** approach recognizes patterns more than parts and looks for connections between them. The logical flow tends to be more circular than linear, and disproving any component part may not invalidate the general claim. Interestingly, cultures at both ends of the spectrum have reasons for finding fault with the logical system of cultures at the other end.

WAYS OF KNOWING

ABSTRACT  CONCRETE

The ways in which ideas are conceptualized and communicated vary from culture to culture in many different ways, including linguistically, which will be considered more in Topic Six. One of the ways in which the treatment of ideas varies is in whether they are rooted abstractly or concretely. **Abstract knowers** tend to think about propositional truths that may not appear directly connected to the physical world. **Concrete knowers** tend to emphasize the observable, and may communicate ideas more relationally by connecting them to stories of readily understood and accessible animals, people, weather, and so on.

NORMS

TIGHT  LOOSE

Cultures have mores and ethical expectations of their members. However, not only do the norms themselves vary from culture to culture. There are also variations in how strictly those norms are enforced within a culture. Some cultures have very strict expectations of adherence to the mores while others expect and allow a certain amount of flexibility and experimentation. These latter cultures can at times be misinterpreted as not having strong morals, but this would tend to be a misjudgment. It could be more accurate to suggest that the morals in such cultures would be perceived as strong enough that tight controls are not needed – that is, that the morals are not threatened by the flexibility around their enforcement. Of course, people from **tight-normed** cultures also have strong reasons for their more rigid enforcement of morals, and neither tight nor **loose-normed** culture should be necessarily interpreted as legalistic or unloving based on only this framework.

SPIRITUALITY

SPIRITUAL IDENTITY  SECULAR IDENTITY

The **spirit world-cosmology** views all of life as existing within a greater spiritual reality. For such cultures, there is a tendency to view the individual identity as ultimately spiritual, though the perceived relationship between the spiritual and the material

can vary significantly even for **spiritual-identity** cultures. **Secular identity** cultures are not necessarily irreligious. However, secular identity cultures tend to view the spiritual world (if they acknowledge it) as separate from the material world. The material world is experienced primarily and the spiritual secondarily if at all. The materialism of such cultures should be understood descriptively rather than evaluative – to say that a culture has a materialistic worldview does not necessarily indicate that people from that culture are consumed with acquisitiveness. Instead it means that the material, rather than the spiritual, is seen as primary. Again, recall that in the spiritual identity perspective the spiritual is not necessarily experienced as primary over the material (though this is an option) – instead it is often viewed as the context in which all material life exists.

 **Discover More!**

There are many books that explore cultural continua. Here are three good starters:

Cross-Cultural Connections by Duane Elmer (2002)

A Beginner's Guide to Crossing Cultures by Patty Lane (2009)

Ministering Cross-Culturally (2nd Ed.) by Sherwood Lingenfelter & Marvin Mayers (2003)

For a more comprehensive book dealing with cultural continua, consider

Hesselgrave's *Communicating Christ Cross-Culturally.*

TOPIC SIX: LANGUAGE AND CULTURE

This section briefly explores the role of language in culture, including both the meaning-making process and the actual communication process.

BIG IDEA #20: LANGUAGE BOTH CONVEYS AND SHAPES MEANING

In considering language, there is often a tendency to assume that different languages are simply different ways to communicate the exact same meaning. From that perspective, translation is simply a matter of taking meaning from one language and finding the words to express the same meaning in another culture.

Anyone who has ever actually done translation can tell you that this simply is not the case. Each language involves its own system of logic and meaning, which may or may not translate well into other languages.

A simple example is the difference between how Spanish and English deal with fault in cases of accidents. In English, for example, a person says "I dropped the plate." To communicate the same event in Spanish a person says "Se me cayó el plato," which more literally translates as "the plate fell itself to me." The English way of communicating the event puts the fault on the individual, whereas the Spanish version reports that the event happened to the individual. On the surface this may appear to be a small difference. After all, both languages report the key fact that the plate has fallen, and that the individual was in some way involved. However, the difference in how the event is communicated reveals differences in the directness or indirectness.

There are a couple of different interpretations of how language and culture influence each other. Several of the most useful of these are related to the Sapir-Whorf hypothesis. Extreme versions of the hypothesis posit that language actually determines the ways in which people think – and in the very extreme even suggesting that it is not possible to think outside of the forms and structures that language has provided. A weaker, and perhaps more helpful version of Sapir-Whorf is that language influences (rather than fully determining) thinking. While there is not agreement among sociolinguists about the extent to which language shapes thought it is clear that the processes that languages use to shape and communicate thoughts can be very different.

One of the key takeaways here is that when interacting with people from different linguistic backgrounds it is appropriate to assume that even when you are using the same language some of the meaning that you and the other person intend to communicate may be lost in translation from your each person's original linguistic system. Interestingly, this can even be the case in communication between speakers of different forms of the same basic language (such as between different versions of English).

BIG IDEA #21: COMMUNICATION IS MORE THAN WORDS

Recall the discussion in Big Idea #5, that communication involves at least two channels – the content channel and the relational channel. Along the same lines, it is important to recognize that communication happens through a variety of mechanisms. This is not an unexpected idea, and in a quote widely (though questionably) attributed to St. Francis of Assisi we find one of the most familiar contemporary Christian comments along these lines: "Speak the gospel, and if necessary use words". As this familiar quote suggests, much more goes into communication than merely the words which are spoken. The remainder of this topic covers several specific areas that can influence the ways in which communication happens beyond merely the words spoken (an area of study called **paralinguistics** describes many of these topics).

These include at least the following:

·   Tonal Differences (Big Idea #22)

·   Word Choice and Word Order (Big Idea #23)

·   Register, Formality and Informality (Big Idea #24)

·   Directness and Indirectness (where the message is found) (Big Idea #25)

·   Emotional Restraint and Emotional Expressiveness (Big Idea #26)

BIG IDEA #22: TONAL DIFFERENCES

Tonal differences refer to distinctions in the ways that people make the sounds with which they speak. These can be reflected in dialectical and accent differences, such as between Bostonians (Massachusetts), Texans, and Californians. Each of these groups has familiar (if stereotyped) accent patterns.

However there are also more nuanced differences to the way tone impacts language. In some language the same sound (**phoneme**) can actually have different meaning if the tone (such as an up or down pitch) is different. Take the Bambara sentence: *N'ba ka ba ba bɛ ba kɔfɛ* for example, which translates as "my mother's big goat is beyond the river" (literally, "Me mother her goat big is river behind."). Ba, depending on the inflection, can mean mother, goat, big, and river.

Tone also communicates important emotional information within groups. For example, you can often tell whether a person is angry, sad, happy, or sarcastic through interpreting their tone. However, this sort of tone does not always translate well. For example, a person who communicates without varying their intonation could be perceived as unemotional or untrustworthy – especially if their tone of voice never varies when discussing a problem with their children. On the other hand, a person whose tone comes across as overly emotive, lazy, or otherwise affected may similarly be distrusted.

Just like interpreting an email, you should always test your linguistic impressions against other data to verify understanding. If the tone of voice doesn't match your expectations, verify understanding. Be very careful using your own inflection to communicate something opposite of your words. Be especially wary of the use of sarcasm with people from other cultural backgrounds, as sarcasm is nearly always signaled by inflection, and may be misinterpreted.

BIG IDEA #23: WORD CHOICE AND WORD ORDER

Word Choice: Word choice can convey meanings that may be other than those that are intended. You may be familiar with one way this plays out through the use of double *entendre*, in which common words and ideas are given sexual, racial, or drug-related second meanings not present in the words themselves. However, this can also go the other way, in which words that obfuscate meaning may be brought into a situation. As an example – the use of the word obfuscate may not be the most appropriate in the context of this introductory book on intercultural competence. The word means "to make unclear or unintelligible," but it was not the best way to express that idea in this context. It is possible to unnecessarily bring division and opportunity for misunderstanding through bringing in words that are not appropriate to the context.

Be aware that your words may have multiple valid interpretations.

BIG IDEA #24: REGISTER, FORMALITY, AND INFORMALITY

Formality and informality in relationship has both linguistic and non-linguistic components.

RELATIONSHIPS

 FORMAL

 INFORMAL

The nature of formality in relationships has direct bearing on the social expression of relationships. Even very close friendships in a **formal relationship** culture may follow regimented patterns of interaction that may appear to outsiders as being cold or distant. **Informal relationship** cultures tend to emphasize fluidity and familiarity that can extend far beyond a person's closest relationships. The interaction between relationally formal and informal cultural members can be particularly awkward in relation to personal space, private possessions, scheduling, topics of conversation, interaction in public spaces, and so forth. What may be perceived as mere friendliness in the informal context may be interpreted as gross over-familiarity or impertinence in the formal context. On the other hand what may be seen as appropriate and respectful in the formal context may be seen as cold, stuffy, or outright unfriendly in the informal context. Formality in relationships can also be expressed linguistically.

In communication between people of the same culture, there are often hidden rules regarding word choice, tempo, and **register**, or varying levels of formality. This is most easily seen when looking at languages that have distinct sets of words built around formal and informal voices. Both Spanish and French, for example have a variation of the "you familiar" (*tu* or *toi*) voice and the "you formal" (*usted* or *vous*) voice. In those languages, when speaking in a formal setting, or to someone older or otherwise more senior than oneself, it is appropriate to use the "you formal" voice. *Tu t'appelles comment?* and *Comment vous appelez-vous?* both mean "What is your name?" (or more literally "What do you call yourself?"), but the first one is in the informal register, while the second is formal.

What may be less immediately obvious are the ways that a similar difference of registers exists within American culture. These registers, or different levels of formality, are very distinct, and the use of the inappropriate register can be a barrier to communication success. Not all English speakers have access to all registers of the English language. The formal register in particular is not always available to many people from certain socioeconomic or ethnic backgrounds where it is not often used. When a person interacts with an authority figure (such as a judge) in an awkwardly informal way (such as by using words like "yeah" "I guess so" or "Uh huh"), this may mean that the person does not have access to the formal register, and may in fact be making an attempt to connect appropriately. Failure to communicate in the formal register should not be interpreted as a lack of intelligence or goodwill.

Familiarize yourself with the registers the people you work with are most likely to use so you don't judge them from a register that they do not have access to.

ACTIVITY 2.13 | TAILORING YOUR MESSAGE

You are a parent of a young child. You want to take time off in a few weeks to attend your sister's wedding. You haven't been getting along well with your boss.

Briefly construct a sentence to communicate the following idea as you would expect it to be communicated in each of the following situations:

Explain to your child that you are planning to go to the wedding.

Explain to your sister that you have to request time off in order to go to the wedding.

Explain to your coworker that you need to take time off in order to go the wedding. She also hasn't been getting along with the boss.

Explain to your boss that you need to take time off to go to the wedding.

In what ways did your sentences vary?

Depending on your own cultural background, you may have come up with very different ways to communicate the same information depending on the people involved. This ability to adapt register is something that you internalize as a member of a culture. For the most part, these rules are not written down.

People from different cultures have different register rules, and they often do not match up. For example, in the US, **people from poverty generally do not have access to the more formal registers**. If you do not have access to a formal register and have to communicate with your boss, how likely is your success as compared with someone who grew up knowing how to use the formal register?

WHAT DO YOU THINK?

How can you help your other people adapt their register when appropriate?

BIG IDEA #25: DIRECT AND INDIRECT COMMUNICATION

Some cultures value **direct communication**, while others value **indirect communication**. Both styles are equally effective in contexts where they are commonly used, but can lead to significant misunderstanding in other contexts.

Direct communicators put their message into words, and aim the words straight at the person who is supposed to receive the message:

Indirect communicators find alternate ways to get their messages across, such as by using a mediator:

Another way indirect communicators get their message across is by talking about something else in a way the hearer will interpret as being about the actual message. Sometimes the words are actually contrary to the message! For example, many times indirect communicators will use words like "yes" when the message is actually "no." This is done to preserve respect for their communication partner.

Test the understanding of the messages you send and receive to verify that the message sent or received was actually the message intended!

AT THE INTERSECTION

"I was once staying with the president of a major church denomination in Mali, when a person from a US ministry called to say he was going to fly in and share some ideas about how his ministry was going to partner with the church. We spent several hours with him and it became increasingly apparent that the church was already doing the kind of training that this visitor's ministry wanted to provide, and that the Malian church was doing the training better than the US organization. My Malian friend, the church president, responded to the visitor by explaining that although the church was really interested in the training that the budget could be a problem.

I didn't immediately recognize the indirect communication and started trying to problem solve the budget issue, even though I knew that my friend was not likely to be interested in the training this visitor was offering. It took me a few minutes to realize that I had interpreted his indirect "no" directly as a "yes, but", and that my attempt to solve his "problem" was actually creating a problem!

Why didn't he just tell the visitor straight out that he wasn't interested? There are several reasons - the first is that he didn't want to embarrass the visitor or cause him problems with his home ministry. The second is that the visitor was a friend of a friend of my Malian friend, and so he did not want to compromise that relationship. The third is that as someone with extensive experience in an indirect culture the visitor should have understood right away that my friend was in fact saying no, even though it sounded like "yes, but we have a challenge". Finally, it was true that the budget would have been a challenge. This, however, was not my friend's primary objection."

- Stephen

 **Discover More!**

There are many books that explore cultural direct and indirect communication. Here is a good starting place:

Cross-Cultural Conflict by Duane Elmer (1994)

AT THE INTERSECTION

Jake and his roommate Brad were having an argument. What began as a normal conversation between the two had turned into a heated discussion. As the argument got more heated, Jake's body language started getting bigger. He started pacing the room and waving his hands about as he attempted to argue his points. Brad got up from the couch and moved to the table in the dining room. Jake followed Brad into the dining room and his tone kept getting louder. Just as the argument was at its peak, Brad told Jake to calm down. Jake stopped pacing, looked at Brad and exited the room, slamming the door behind him. Brad stared blankly after Jake, confused at what just happened.

BIG IDEA #26: EMOTIONAL RESTRAINT AND EMOTIONAL EXPRESSIVENESS

As mentioned previously, there are multiple channels at play in any communication between people. The first has to do with the *what* – the issue that is being discussed. The second has to do with the question of *how are we* – the relational status.

One of the ways that relational status is communicated is through the use of **emotional restraint** or **emotional expression**.

 ACTIVITY 2.14 | EMOTION IN COMMUNICATION

Below you will find a list of things a person might do in a conflict situation. Next to each item, indicate whether the behavior would make you feel more or less comfortable about the status of the relationship, by circling the **thumbs up** (more comfortable), the **circle** (no real effect), the **thumbs down** (less comfortable) or the **warning sign** (might escalate to violence).

👍⭕👎⚠ The person you are arguing with starts to use large, animated gestures.

👍⭕👎⚠ The person you are arguing with makes an obvious shift toward being quiet and controlled. He/she is being very deliberate about what words to use.

👍⭕👎⚠ The person you are arguing with begins to close up physically, creating increased distance and 'blocking you out' such as by crossing his/her arms.

👍⭕👎⚠ The person you are arguing with starts to speak faster and louder, accessing a broader range of language and metaphors than normal, including curses and insults.

👍⭕👎⚠ The person you are arguing with backs away and starts to mumble.

👍⭕👎⚠ The person you are arguing with uses an object on the table or bar to articulate a point.

👍⭕👎⚠ The person you are arguing with starts to use very formal and structured language.

👍⭕👎⚠ The person you are arguing with makes a verbal threat of violence

Overall, would you say that emotional expression or emotional restraint tends to make you more uncomfortable in conflict?

One of the sometimes baffling things about emotional expression and restraint is that the same action can have two completely different meanings, depending on the cultural norms. For example, emotionally restrained cultures would tend to view number two, becoming more controlled, as positive (or at least neutral), because it is a sign that the other person is making an effort to preserve the relationship.

However, emotionally expressive cultures would tend to view that same action as an escalation of the conflict, because it demonstrates, in that view, a lack of commitment and/or evasiveness.

This same kind of mismatch is true for each of the above items! Consider number 8 -- in emotionally expressive cultures, verbal threats of violence are often not considered to be actual threats. They are instead considered to be part of the conflict negotiation process. For example, if an emotionally expressive person threatens to punch you in the face, this may just be part of a game or verbal battle by which the two of you figure out how serious you are about the conflict. However, an emotionally restrained person will tend to view this as an imminent threat of violence and may therefore act preemptively, thus initiating a violent confrontation based on a misperceived threat of actual violence.

TOPIC SEVEN: INTERCULTURAL CONFLICT STYLES

Continuing our Unit 2 Goal of *seeing culture*, it is helpful to examine core **conflict styles**. Different cultures have norms about how to handle conflict. As was discussed in the preceding pages, some cultures rely on **direct** expression of the conflict issue (what the problem is about), whereas others emphasize a more **indirect** method for handling conflict, where the specific issue may never be overtly addressed. Cultures also very in the levels of **emotional restraint** or **emotional expression** considered to be appropriate for people from different cultures. In some cultures, emotional expression (loudness, large gestures, increasingly creative and sometimes increasingly vulgar vocabulary) build increased trust. In other cultures, those same behaviors may destroy emotional trust.

It is important to understand that within each culture, the core conflict style is effective. Within indirect cultures, for example, people know to look for messages outside of the specific words that are spoken. Because everyone in those cultures knows that the message is outside of the specific words, this method is effective and is not lying – even it if would be in a direct communication culture.

BIG IDEA #27: DIRECTNESS AND INDIRECTNESS INTERSECT WITH EMOTIONAL EXPRESSION AND RESTRAINT

There are four major potential combinations available between these four conflict modes:

DIRECT & EMOTIONALLY RESTRAINED

DIRECT & EMOTIONALLY EXPRESSIVE

INDIRECT & EMOTIONALLY RESTRAINED

INDIRECT & EMOTIONALLY EXPRESSIVE

It is important to note that while there are four main modes, each with its own norms and tendencies, that there are also **variations within each style**. When interacting with people from one's own style, the differences within the style may feel just as significant as if you were interacting with someone from a different style.

For example, majority culture Americans tend to be direct and emotionally restrained. If a person (represented by the blue star) is extremely direct and emotionally restrained, they might have as much difficulty interacting with someone who is in less direct and more expressive but still within same overall style as them (represented by the green star) as they would interacting with someone who is actually indirect and expressive (represented by the purple star).

That is to say, sometimes the relative difference between people can be just as important in communication difficulties as people's overall styles. One of the important effects of this reality is that you may have conflict with someone who is culturally similar to you but is relatively more or less direct or expressive than you. If you are experiencing conflict, try analyzing it using this model and see if it helps to explain your frustration.

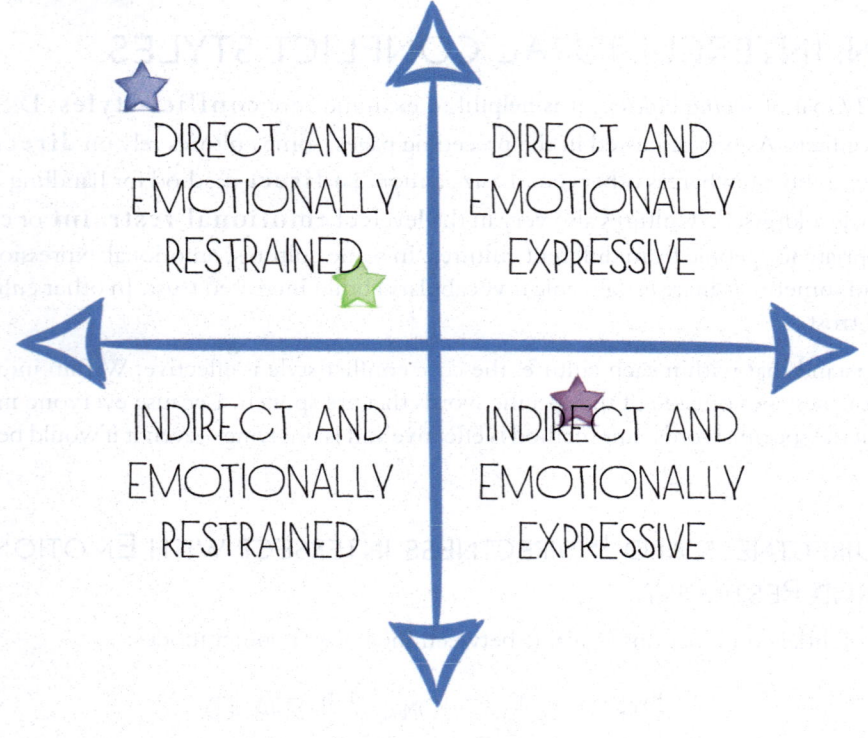

DIRECT AND EMOTIONALLY RESTRAINED

DIRECT AND EMOTIONALLY EXPRESSIVE

INDIRECT AND EMOTIONALLY RESTRAINED

INDIRECT AND EMOTIONALLY EXPRESSIVE

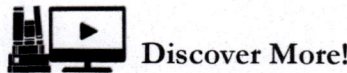 **Discover More!**

Keep Learning: Take the Intercultural Conflict Styles (ICS) Inventory! Find out more at:

www.thepracticalinterculturalist.com/howtointercultural

WHAT DO YOU THINK?

What was your intercultural conflict style (ICS) on the ICS Inventory?

Did you already realize this about yourself or was this basically new information?

Which style is the hardest for you to get along with? Why?

How might differences in conflict styles impact those you work with?

How can you become more flexible in interacting with other peoples' conflict styles?

SUMMARY

INTERACTING WITH CULTURE | 3

"It is no wonder—in our time of mass migrations and culture collisions and easy jet travel, when the whole world lies below us every time we rise into the skies, when whole countries move by like bits of checkerboard, ours to play on—it's no wonder that in this time we've developed whole philosophies of cultural relativity, and learned to look at whole literatures, histories, and cultural formations as if they were toy blocks, ours to construct and deconstruct.

It's no wonder, also, that we have devised a whole metaphysics for the subjects of difference and otherness. But for all our sophisticated deftness at cross-cultural encounters, fundamental difference, when it's staring at you across the table from within the close-up face of a fellow human being, always contains an element of violation."

Eva Hoffman, Lost in Translation, *1990, pp. 209-210*

Hoffman's quote, if uncomfortable, is also incredibly true. Cultural difference is something that you can adapt to, that you can become good at navigating, and that you can enjoy. Yet there is something inescapably disturbing about the realization that people really do live, think, and perceive the world differently from the way that you do.

That element of discomfort, although at times unwelcome, is also a tremendous teacher. In **Unit One** we considered how people doing life together make decisions in patterns that we call *culture*. In **Unit Two** we explored cultural frameworks that we can use to explore those patterns.

In this unit, we continue the intercultural journey by considering what to expect when we come into contact with other cultures. To do this, we will explore several topics that are important in order to understand both your own interaction with other cultures, as well as the experiences of those you work with.

In **Topic Eight**, we begin with a brief overview of the role of **identity** in intercultural relationships. This is a very complex topic, and we will only cover a few basics.

Topic Nine introduces the idea of **reflexive skills**. These are ways in which you can take ownership of your experience when in a cross-cultural setting.

Topic Ten introduces **ethnographic skills** that can be used to record the multi-channeled realities of life as they happen, to provide fuller engagement with the clients' realities than is possible at first.

Topic Eleven explores the stages of **transition** relevant to any major life change, along with the specific challenges of interacting with cross-cultural transitions, such as culture shock and reentry shock.

Topic Twelve is an introduction to a stage model of **intercultural development** that you may find helpful in understanding both your own interaction with cultural difference and the interactions that your clients have with cultural difference.

TOPIC EIGHT: IDENTITY

Identity, as we are using the term, refers to how a person understands who he or she is. This is affected by everything that makes a person: family background, birth order, physical and genetic composition, ethnicity and race, physical and mental health, morality, nation, region, state, city, occupation, spirituality, religion, relational status, age, generation, hobbies and activities, politics, and more. There is, in fact, no simple way to explain your own identity, or the identity of someone else.

We begin this Topic, then, with three activities designed to explore different elements of your identity.

In **Activity 3.1**, we begin by trying to decide which elements of your identity are the most important.

In **Activity 3.2**, we look at how elements of your identity intersect with each other.

Finally, in **Activity 3.3**, we explore how your identity is impacted by both internal and external factors.

 **Discover More!**

Want to start with a book? Read about ethnic identity in the US:

 *Being White: Finding Our Place in a Multiethnic World*. by Paula Harris and Doug Schaupp. Downers Grove, Ill: InterVarsity Press, 2004.

 ACTIVITY 3.1 | WHO ARE YOU?

Who are you? Make a list with at least twenty responses.

If you did not include your gender, age, religion, and ethnicity/race, go back and add those now.

How difficult was it for you to come up with responses?

Were you surprised by how easy or difficult it was to make this list?

Now go back and circle the items that you would consider to be long-term. Then, having selected which items you feel are permanent, copy them into these lists, leaving the box to the left of each column blank:

	PERMANENT		TEMPORARY

Now go back to the list you just made and rank order the items in each list in terms of what is most important to you, placing the number ranking in the appropriate box, as shown here:

Permanent		Temporary	
2	Friend	1	Student
1	Daughter	2	Athlete

Having done that, now recopy your top 5 permanent items and top 5 temporary items:

PERMANENT		TEMPORARY	
1		1	
2		2	
3		3	
4		4	
5		5	

WHAT DO YOU THINK?

What did you find difficult about this exercise? What information does that give you?

Did you originally include your gender, age, religion, & race/ethnicity? What information does your initial decision to include or not include these elements reveal to you?

Ranking these items in terms of importance to you is called creating a "salience hierarchy." Why might it be good to know which items are most salient to you?

For you, would you say that your salience hierarchy changes depending on what situation you are in? Why or why not?

Why might it be important to be aware of your identity salience hierarchy?

BIG IDEA #28: IDENTITY IS COMPLICATED

As you may have recognized in the Activity 3.1, identity is complicated. There are several reasons for this.

- ✠   Identity is formed in response to both **internal attributes and external inputs.**
- ✠   Individual Identity is developed in response to multiple inputs, including **family and social settings,** and this is accomplished largely through communication with others.
- ✠   Identity can **fluctuate** depending on life changes (both aspirational and actual).

"Cultural identities are negotiated, co-created, reinforced, and challenged through communication." - (Collier, 1997 in Orbe & Harris, 2001, p. 95)

ACTIVITY 3.2 | IDENTITY WEB

On this page, create an identity web with the items from the short list you came up with in Activity 3.1. Place permanent items on the round web lines, and the temporary items on the radiating lines. There is an example on the next page. Be sure to include your race/ethnicity and gender.

After adding your identity items, then go back and label the intersections using symbols like these:

Means that for you, the intersection between these elements of your identity is positive.

Means that for you, the intersection between these elements of your identity is neutral.

Means that for you, the intersection between these elements of your identity is challenging.

In this example, notice that the intersection of 'permanent 3' and 'temporary 2' is labeled as a challenge, the intersection of 'permanent 3' and 'temporary 2' is labeled as neutral, and the intersection of 'permanent 2' and 'temporary 3' is labeled as positive.

Once you have completed labeling each intersection, total the number of each symbol that you used.

How many positive intersections? _____

How many neutral intersections? _____

How many challenging intersections? _____

Which parts of your identity had the most positive intersections? Why do you think that is?

Which parts of your identity had the most challenging intersections? Why do you think that is?

What other insights did you gain from this exercise?

If you did an exercise like this with one of your parents, siblings, classmates, or with a person you work with, what might you learn about their perspective?

BIG IDEA #29: IDENTITY CAN BE CONTESTED

Identity, as you have seen, is complicated. But it can also be **contested**, because **internal and external identity may conflict with each other**.

Huang (2003) suggests that there are two major components of a person's identity: Internal, and External.

The **internal identity** is comprised of both ethnic and non-ethnic identifications that a person holds. The elements that make up a person's internal identity may not always be consistent and may not always be things that a person likes about his or herself. However, they are recognizable because they are consistently influential in the person's identity. The point in the internal identity section is to identify what you think about yourself, regardless of whether it is consistent and, at this stage, without evaluation.

The **external identity** is comprised of both ascribed in-groups (what groups people say you are a part of) and out-groups (what groups you are not a part of), and the relationship between these. Like the internal identity, these do not necessarily have to be consistent. For example, there are some people who will find certain elements of their identity on both the ascribed in-groups and the outgroups list. Even weirder, sometimes elements on the ascribed in groups list will not match at all with the internal identity. Other times, they will mirror it very closely. The point in the external identity section is to identify what others say, regardless of whether it is accurate or consistent.

Ultimately, these internal and external identities come together to form a person's identity. This identity can be **cohesive, challenged, or fractured** (among other possibilities), as well as **positive or negative** or anywhere in between. This identity can also be **static** and consistent, or **dynamic** and changing.

ACTIVITY 3.3 | HUANG'S IDENTITY DEVELOPMENT MODEL

Fill out these components for yourself:

Ethnic Identifications	Non-Ethnic Identifications
1.	1.
2.	2.
3.	3.
4.	4.
5.	5.

Now bring these together to form an identity salience hierarchy (review Big Idea #28 if you need a refresher)

1.

2.

3.

4.

5.

The list you just made is the Personal Internal Identity. Now work on the Social External Identity. Make a list of which groups people assume you are a member of (ascribed in-group) and what groups are not a part of, or assumed not to be a part of (out-groups). In some cases the same groups may appear in both of these lists

Ascribed In-Group	Out-Groups
1.	1.
2.	2.
3.	3.
4.	4.
5.	5.

Now consider the social relationships between the in-groups and out-groups. For example, if you are assumed to be black, and assumed not to be Hispanic, what are the relationships between those groups in your normal context – do they interact? Are those interactions positive, negative, both?

Your answer above provides an exploration the intergroup relations. Now we want to bring everything together, by considering the personal internal identity and the social external identity together. What happens when you bring them together? Are they consistent? Are there distinctions between them?

Sum up your identity in one phrase or sentence, incorporating both the internal and external identity:

Having summed up your identity, describe your experience of your identity:

examples: "I have a contested, positive, integrated identity because although people misinterpret my ethnicity, I understand how the components of my identity relate, and I like my overall identity" or "disintegrated, negative, affirmed identity, because my ethnicity and religion do not fit well together, but people usually interpret me accurately—I wish they wouldn't, because I don't like being part of this group."

WHAT DO YOU THINK?

What in this model was new for you?

What did you learn about yourself?

How might this exercise help you learn about someone else's experiences in the world? If you are working with a group or class, consider sharing your identity model with someone else to compare your experience.

How could you use this model to help someone else navigate their social situation?

BIG IDEA #30: CIRCUMSTANCE AFFECTS IDENTITY NEGOTIATION

Identity negotiation is a more or less constant process for nearly all people. However, there are several circumstances that can cause people to find identity negotiation to be particularly important or challenging:

* Ongoing minority status

* Sudden change in majority / minority status

* Cross-cultural relocation as an expatriate, immigrant, or refugee

* Child of an expatriate, immigrant, or refugee

* Disrupted family status

Let's explore each of these briefly.

Ongoing minority status can cause significant distress in the identity negotiation process. Every society has certain non-dominant groups that are regularly reminded of their outsider status. In the US, minority groups include most non-white groups, non-English speakers, recent immigrants, the poor, the homeless, and the disabled among others. In certain settings, women have also been treated as a marginalized out-group. There are daily reminders to members of these groups that society was not built for them.

Although it can be appropriate to analyze this situation through the lens of social justice, this present section is intended only to raise your awareness to the reality that living in a society that is not built for you can force regular reflection on identity.

Consider a these examples from Peggy McIntosh, who realized that although she was part of a challenged group as a woman that she was also part of privileged group as a White American.

1. I can if I wish arrange to be in the company of people of my race most of the time.

2. I can go shopping alone most of the time, pretty well assured that I will not be followed or harassed.

3. I can turn on the television or open to the front page of the paper and see people of my race widely represented.

4. When I am told about our national heritage or about "civilization," I am shown that people of my color made it what it is.

5. I can go into a music shop and count on finding the music of my race represented, into a supermarket and find the staple foods which fit with my cultural traditions, into a hairdresser's shop and find someone who can cut my hair.

6. I can do well in a challenging situation without being called a credit to my race.

7. I am never asked to speak for all the people of my racial group.

8. If a traffic cop pulls me over or if the IRS audits my tax return, I can be sure I haven't been singled out because of my race.

9. I can easily buy posters, postcards, picture books, greeting cards, dolls, toys, and children's magazine featuring people of my race.

10. I can take a job with an affirmative action employer without having co-workers on the job suspect that I got it because of race.

11. I can choose blemish cover or bandages in "flesh" color and have them more or less match my skin.

How could being outside of the majority group impact a person's identity?

McIntosh's list focuses on race. How might being part of other minority groups affect someone's identity?

Sudden change in minority / majority status can also cause challenges in identity negotiation. For example, if a person is used to being a visible minority group member and suddenly finds his or herself in the visible majority, this can actually cause an identity disorientation. Similarly, going from being a visible majority group member to being a visible minority can be very unsettling. In either case, a person develops certain ways to interpret their relative invisibility or visibility as part of his or her identity. A change in visibility impacts those elements of the identity, sometimes profoundly.

Cross-cultural relocation as an expatriate, immigrant, or refugee can be one of the most profound challenges to identity negotiation. One of the most important reasons for this challenge is that the much of a person's identity is reinforced by his or her local setting and patterns. Cross-cultural relocation disrupts the regular affirmation of identity. It does not matter whether the disrupted identity was positive, negative, contested, or otherwise – the process of identity disruption is always significantly challenging.

This identity disruption is particularly difficult for immigrants who hold degrees in their home country that are not recognized in the US. For example, consider a doctor or lawyer from South America whose medical education is not recognized in America, and who can only find work doing after-hours office cleaning.

Refugees of various kinds also face significant identity disruption. Many times refugees did not want to leave their home country, but were forced out due to a significantly unsettling event. Refugee status in the US can provide a safe-haven, but a refugee's heart may still be in his or her home country. What's more, refugees have often lost access to family members (which always impacts identity) either through death or through travel restrictions that prevent them from returning home.

 **Discover More!**

For additional reading on the immigrant and refugee experience check out the following books:

 *Mary Pipher's The Middle of Everywhere: Helping Refugees Enter the American Community*

 *Matthew Soerens' and Jenny Hwang Yang's Welcoming the Stranger*

Children of expatriates, immigrants, or refugees have their own unique challenges. Generally, being the child of someone from somewhere else is called being a "Third Culture Kid" (TCK for short). Their parents may be living in a place other than their birth-land because of business, the military, missionary or service work, or because they are immigrants or refugees. Third culture kids do not identify as strongly with their "original" culture as their parents do, because their participation in that culture is limited due to living elsewhere. At the same time, TCKs are outsiders in their new home culture. The third culture that TCKs inhabit is in between their parents' culture and the host culture.

It is important to note that in some cases TCKs can be particularly vulnerable to the influence of those who do not have their best interest at heart. The children of immigrants and refugees are sometimes targeted for inclusion in gangs who tap into the child's desire to fit in and find a stable identity. Gangs, despite all their dysfunction, offer an identity for immigrant and refugee children.

 **Discover More!**

For additional reading on TCK's, the leading author is the late David Pollock. Check out:

 *David Pollock's and R. Van Reken's (2011) Third culture kids: Growing up among worlds.*

Disrupted family status can also greatly affect identity formation and maintenance, both in children and adults. Children's primary reference group is their immediate family (not necessarily the nuclear family – but the family members who raise them). When there is a disruption due to displacement (i.e. incarceration, removal from the home, moving for a job, etc.), divorce, or death (among other causes), this can affect the way every member of the family sees his or herself in relation not only to the family, but to the larger world. These effects can be both for good and for bad, but they are always disruptive to identity. In response to this identity disruption some people (both adults and children) will act out in various ways in attempts to recover the identity they previously had, even if it was negative.

It is important to recognize that even efforts to help people and their families are necessarily threatening to identity. It is important to recognize that many well-meaning social service and ministry organizations do work that intends to *interrupt the family system*. That interruption is, of course, both intended and designed to bring benefit to the family. The fact remains that this kind of work will challenge previously understood roles and identity within the family system, and organizations that do this kind of work must be very intentional about being ethical in their service to the community.

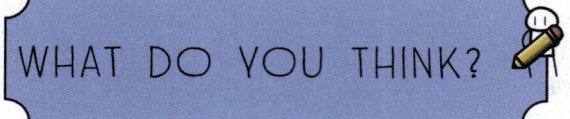

WHAT DO YOU THINK?

How would it impact your understanding of your role and identity if an outside organization started trying to change the way your family (or a member of your family) did life?

There are *two more issues* that you should be familiar with in terms of understanding identity.

Hypodescent refers to the cultural belief that if a child has a white and a non-white parent, the child is non-white. At its extremes, any non-white heritage is enough to "disqualify" a person from the white majority in America (this is also called the one-drop rule). Although some significant progress has been made toward the recognition of bi-racial heritage, hypodescent is

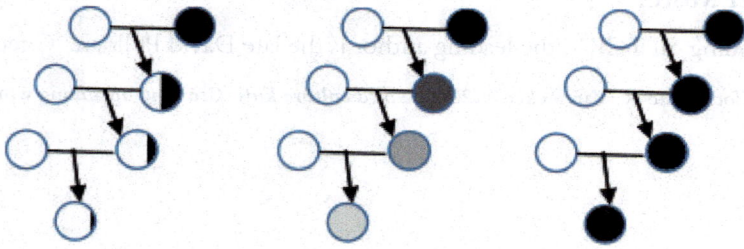

still the *de facto* interpretation of racial heritage in America. The roots of this belief are of course not biological but cultural, with a significant heritage in the slavery and Jim Crow segregation of the past.

In the image below, if each dot is a parent, either the left or center descent trees would make sense in explaining the biological contributions of each parent. However, it is the third descent tree that is used in the rule of hypodescent, where only the racial contribution of the non–white parent "counts".

Proximal host refers to the group that a person is assumed to be a member of, based on which groups are locally present. For example, many Haitians have been assumed to be African-American because of the similar **phenotype**. However, Haitians do not share the African-American history or cultural patterns, so it is simply incorrect to call Haitians African-American. The issue of proximal host can apply to any outsider – for example, White Canadians may be assumed to be Minnesotan. This may also explain some of the results you found in the social external identity portion of Activity 3.3.

BIG IDEA #31: IDENTITY DEVELOPMENT OFTEN FOLLOWS PREDICTABLE PATTERNS

There are many models of ethnic identity development, each of which emphasizes different elements of the process of negotiating identity in a contested setting. One such model is offered by Sue and Sue (1999). Sue and Sue identified *five common stages* of racial/cultural identity development. For non-dominant group members these are as follows:

1. **Conformity** to the majority culture, including negative evaluations of a person's own minority group.

2. **Resistance** to the previously held attachment to the majority culture.

3. **Dissonance and Immersion** is a stage of rejecting the majority culture and identification with the minority culture.

4. **Introspection** causes a person to recognize the unhealthiness of completely rejecting majority culture.

5. **Integrative Awareness** is a stage in which a person is able to balance appreciation (and critique) of both majority and minority culture.

 **Discover More!**

There is a lot more to learn about identity negotiation! Consider reading:

 *Race Ethnicity and Self edited by Elizabeth Pathy Salett and Diane R. Koslow (2003).*

This book includes Huang's identity model (originally conceptualized for Asian Americans), along with considerations of the development of African American, Native American, Puerto Rican, White, Biracial, Native American, and Vietnamese identity development.

TOPIC NINE: REFLEXIVE SKILLS

BIG IDEA #32: YOU ARE NOT NEUTRAL

As you interact across cultures, one of the important skills relates to taking ownership of your experience in the cross-cultural setting. Consider this – as you navigate cross-cultural situations, you are never neutral. This lack of neutrality comes from several sources:

❋ Your own previous personal and professional experiences

❋ Active or latent prejudices

❋ Your own emotional, physical, and spiritual well-being

❋ External pressures

❋ Situational factors

It is important that you recognize your lack of neutrality especially if you are in a role that involves helping others. It is impossible to be completely objective, so rather than attempt that, your goal should be to notice your subjectivity, record it, and call it into question as appropriate.

ACTIVITY 3.4 | RECOGNIZING SUBJECTIVITY

Consider this situation:

Elizabeth is a dedicated case worker in a large city. She was recently assigned a case in which a child is being considered for reunification with his family. The father is in prison on drug charges, but is expected out within the next year. The mother works two jobs. As Elizabeth begins investigating the case she is disturbed by the similarity to another case she heard about, where the father returned home and was both verbally and physically abusive. Having been physically abused as a child, Elizabeth is very sensitive to these situations.

Before she has had a chance to meet the boy and his mother, Elizabeth receives three more unrelated cases. This has been happening more and more due to recent budget cuts, and the stress of work is really piling up. It doesn't help that her domineering supervisor keeps pushing for faster turnaround times, and doesn't seem to care about protecting the kids in the system. The supervisor is too much like her stupid ex-husband. Speaking of which, he hasn't sent this month's child support.

When she finally has the opportunity to do a site visit at the mother's house, Elizabeth's nose is struck with the acrid stench of old urine. She didn't have time to eat breakfast and only had a granola bar for lunch, so the smell really turns her stomach.

The mother has completed all requirements for reunification, but is consistently evasive when it comes to questions about the father. Elizabeth remembers her own mom not wanting to let anyone know about the abuse in her house growing up, and is really frustrated with the mother for not just coming clean about what she is facing.

Elizabeth is working with a third party provider in the reunification process, but she hasn't had a chance to review the notes (too much detail) sent by that case worker. Ultimately she denies the reunification request in the interest of protecting the child from his potentially abusive father.

Reread the case and circle the elements that were external to the case but might have been affecting Elizabeth as she interacted with the situation.

Of course the issue of being affected by externals is not restricted to any particular group, such as the groups of which Elizabeth is a member. This is a challenge for **everyone**!

Good steps to take include:

1. Acknowledge that you not neutral.

2. Recognize the externalities that are impacting you.

3. As you consider a particular situation, take time to reflect on what you might be bringing to the situation.

4. It can be especially helpful to journal or otherwise record the externalities that you are bringing to a situation – especially one where you have authority over others - so you can review your decision making process to check for accuracy.

5. The goal is not to become objective (you can't) instead the goal is to recognize and where possible mitigate your subjectivity.

6. This does not mean that intuition and past experience should not guide you, but that you should recognize the times and ways in which this is happening.

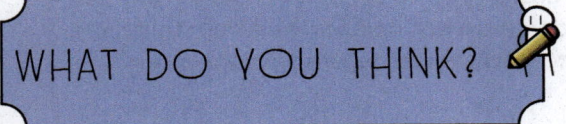

WHAT DO YOU THINK?

Can you think of times when you have realized that you are not as neutral as you thought you were? How have you handled it?

BIG IDEA #33: YOU CAN LEAD YOURSELF

Interacting with people across cultures can be tremendous fun, an exhilarating challenge, an opportunity for powerful partnerships, and an eye-opening adventure. Yet interacting with people across cultures can also be disappointingly slow, full of hidden surprises, and generally much more difficult and laborious than you want it to be – like any true adventure, the cross-cultural life has moments of incredible highs, frightening lows, and a lot of reality that must be waded through on a daily basis.

As you pursue this journey, it is important to recognize that you are actually a powerful participant in the cross-cultural encounter. You may not be able to understand why others think, say, or do what they do, but you do have the opportunity to *lead yourself* in the intercultural encounter. There are a number of different methodologies for attempting this, but one of the most powerful methods that interculturalists have developed is called, appropriately enough, *personal leadership*.

Schaetti, Ramsey, and Watanabe (2008) developed **personal leadership** as a methodology to help facilitate successful cross-cultural interaction. The two guiding principles are **mindfulness** and **creativity**.

 **Discover More!**

Although the method is briefly introduced here, it is highly recommended that you stop and read the following book:

 Personal leadership: Making a world of difference: a methodology of two principles and six practices. By Schaetti,B.F., Ramsey, S. J., & Watanabe, G. C. (2008). Seattle, WA: FlyingKite Publications.

A quick note about the *Personal Leadership* book – some American Christians may find some of the language and the framing of the ideas in the *Personal Leadership* book to be unfamiliar or uncomfortable. That is ok! You can experience this book as a cross-cultural excursion itself! There are some excellent principles in the book that are very useful, and you do not need to be afraid to access them. Disregard what is unhelpful, but I would particularly encourage you to appreciate the intentions and insights of the authors.

Mindfulness involves being fully aware of how you are interacting with a situation. There is a significant difference between getting angry without recognizing it and being aware that you are getting angry. In the second state, the mindful anger, you have the opportunity to interrogate your anger and find out what might be causing it, which in turn allows you to take active leadership of your anger. This allows you to, in the moment, redirect your emotions and responses toward more constructive ends. As followers of Jesus, mindfulness is also a way in which we can reflect on whether we are listening to and being responsive to the Holy Spirit.

Creativity is closely related, in that creativity allows you to determine alternative interpretations for the events you experience, as well as to actively craft your own responses so as to achieve the best possible outcome. One of the important steps to moving toward **personal leadership** is determining what your optimum participation in the cross-cultural encounter will be. This is accomplished though the creation of a vision statement.

ACTIVITY 3.5 | PERSONAL LEADERSHIP VISION

Reread chapter eight of ***Personal Leadership*** by Schaetti, et al. As you seek to create the vision statement, remember that it should be Personal, Powerful, Present, and Positive. At the same time, your vision will be the most useful if it emphasizes a being (rather than a doing) orientation. In terms of context, try to go a little beyond your professional context and think about how you contribute to the human experience generally (though, of course that could include being an excellent professional).

Go ahead and begin crafting a personal vision statement. Begin with the words below:

At my Holy-Spirit empowered best I . . .

Now go back and read your vision. Is it personal? Powerful? Present? Positive? Avoid using negations (like "I am not bad at what I do"). Does this vision inspire you?

Here is a sample vision statement:

At my Holy Spirit empowered best, I actively and intentionally represent Christ in my interactions with all people. I represent the truth of Jesus through my commitment to Holy-Spirit empowered excellence and Jesus-centered gentleness. I boldly (but gently) engage the pain of individuals and of society, looking to redeem this pain for the sake of the Kingdom. I walk closely with the Holy Spirit, relying on His power, and moving in His strength. I confess my sins and both receive and believe in the forgiveness Jesus extends to me, and I extend forgiveness to others because of Him. I honor the image of God in all people, both those who are similar and different, and am an active part of the work of reconciliation of people with each other and with God.

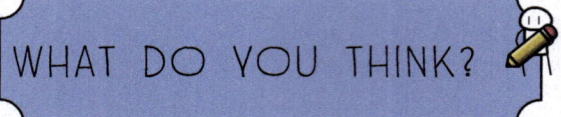

WHAT DO YOU THINK?

What did you find interesting in this vision statement? What did you resonate with?

Do you need to make any changes to your statement to make it more personal, powerful, present, or positive?

CRITICAL MOMENT DIALOGUE

In the book, you became familiar with the six practices of Personal Leadership, which culminate in a process called the Critical Moment Dialogue. Consider the following fictitious adapted example of a completed Critical Moment Dialogue.

First, describe the Critical Moment. Make sure to focus in on a particular moment so that you can be specific in your reflections.

I was sitting out front with some of my friends – some of us were from America and some of us were from the host country where we were staying for awhile. At some point a lady walked past us without saying hi, which was really unusual, because people always say hi. Instead, she walked past us to the house back behind the house we were sitting at – the way the compound was set up it was hard to get to that house without walking by this one first. She evidently couldn't find that family that lived at the second house and came back to the first house where we were and asked where the other family was. I was really shocked when my host-dad said that he didn't know where the other family was, because I knew that he did know. The lady left without my host-dad ever fessing up that he did know where they were.

Attending to Judgment

1. What is the positive or negative judgment I am having about myself, or the situation or person I am facing?
I am making a really negative judgement about my host-dad because he lied to the lady. I can't believe he did that! What's worse is that he is a church leader and people should be able to trust him. Now I'm wondering if he lies all the time – does he lie to me?

I'm also judging myself. It seems like I should have said something in the moment because I know that he was lying and I let him get away with it.

2. What positive or negative assumptions am I making about myself, the other, or the situation?
I assume that my host dad knows it's wrong to lie. I also am assuming that I understood what happened. I guess I might be making an assumption about the lady that was looking for the family, but I don't really know what it would be.

3. What was I expecting? What positive or negative motivations am I attributing to myself and any others involved?
I was expecting my host dad to tell the truth! I am attributing a negative motivation to my host dad – that he intended to deceive the woman. I am attributing a negative motivation to myself – that I was too chicken to say something.

Attending to Emotion

4. What is the emotion, positive or negative, that I am having in this situation?
I'm really angry with my host dad. I'm also really upset with myself because I didn't stand up for something.

5. What are its qualities and characteristics?
It's kind of a sad anger – not so much a fierce one.

6. What information is the emotion offering me?

I think that my anger is showing me that I'm also a little scared because I don't know whether or not I can trust my host dad.

7. Why do I care about this situation so much; which of my values are involved?

Part of why I care is because it's wrong to lie, and it seems to me that every Christian should know that – especially a church leader! What kind of witness does this guy have if he is telling lies!?!

Another part of why I care so much is because I have to rely on my host dad for most of how I survive here. Now that I don't know if I can trust him I feel really frustrated and scared.

Attending to Physical Sensation

8. What is the physical sensation I'm experiencing in this "critical moment" situation; where is the sensation located?

I have a knot in my stomach. My jaw is clenched. My shoulders are tight. My fists keep clenching up when I think about it and I am starting to get a headache.

Also – I'm suddenly really tired.

9. What is the sensation about; what is it communicating to me

I think it's telling me that this is a really big deal to me. My body is telling me that I feel threatened and angry. I think it is also telling me that it's going to be hard for me to sort this out while I'm so tired.

10. What do I need to do to re-establish balance in my body?

I probably need to sleep, but I don't know if I can. I wish I was allowed to go for a run, because that would help me to blow off some steam. I feel too distracted to pray. I feel like watching a movie and just forgetting about it but the power is out. Maybe I'll go for a walk in the garden (hopefully the snakes aren't out). It's funny but even just thinking through the options of what I could do I'm starting to realize that all I really want to do is to sleep. I think a nap will really help me.

Cultivating Stillness

11. What additional questions do I need to ask about judgment, emotion, and the way that I am feeling?

I guess I'm realizing that there's a lot bugging me beside my host-dad lying. I wonder how long I've been bothered by these things.

12. Taking a breath, what insight comes from being quiet and still?

One of the things that comes to me is that I don't know that lady at all but that I do know my host-dad and that so far he hasn't let me down in any way that really matters.

13. What can I learn about myself from this "critical moment" situation? What can I learn about God from this "critical moment" situation?

One think that I'm realizing about myself is that it is really important to me to be able to trust other people. I kind of knew that, but now I really am seeing it in a new way.

The other thing that I'm realizing is that so much about life is hard right now and I'm kind of angry with God because of it. I think maybe I've been hiding from being aware of that.

14. What might the Holy Spirit be trying to say to me or lead me toward or away from?
It's weird, but this question actually made me kind of mad when I saw it. I think that means that I feel kind of far from God right now. I feel like He's trying to show me that and that He wants me to trust Him.

Engaging Ambiguity

15. What do I not know?
Like I said, I actually don't know anything about that lady. I don't know why she was looking for that family. I don't know whether my host dad knows her. I don't know what her character is like.

16. What more can I not know? (Think of examples of things that you thought you knew, but really did not know)
I guess I don't know if my host dad thought he was lying. I don't know whether there is some cultural explanation that would explain why he appeared to be lying. I also don't know what would have happened if I had tried to confront him while the lady was there.

17. What can I do to get more comfortable with the ambiguity and/or to get some clarification?
I think I could probably ask my host dad or one of our other hosts who was there when the event happened.

Aligning with Vision

First, copy your vision statement here:
At my Holy Spirit empowered best, I actively and intentionally represent Christ in my interactions with all people. I represent the truth of Jesus through my commitment to Holy-Spirit empowered excellence and Jesus-centered gentleness. I boldly (but gently) engage the pain of individuals and of society, looking to redeem this pain for the sake of the Kingdom. I walk closely with the Holy Spirit, relying on His power, and moving in His strength. I confess my sins and both receive and believe in the forgiveness Jesus extends to me, and I extend forgiveness to others because of Him. I honor the image of God in all people, both those who are similar and different, and am an active part of the work of reconciliation of people with each other and with God.

18. Where are the gaps between my current reality and the vision statement I wrote about myself at Spirit-empowered best?
I definitely don't feel like I've been walking closely with the Holy Spirit or relying on His strength. I also was much quicker to judge than I was to think about extending forgiveness to someone else. I don't feel like I was very gentle, but I also wasn't bold.

19. What aspects of my vision are confirmed by my reflection on this "critical moment" situation or interaction?
I think this actually confirms a lot in my vision statement – especially the things that I felt like I wasn't doing in #18.

20. How, if at all, does this "critical moment" experience suggest I change/refine my vision?
I think it might be good if I add something about waiting to judge until I have more information.

Discerning Right Action

21. What might I do to bring my current reality into alignment with my vision?

I probably need to ask more about what happened. I think my host-dad would be open to it. I also need to rest.

I think I'm also realizing that I need to open myself up to the work of the Spirit in me today. I didn't realize I was so distant from Him until I started going through this.

22. What does it look like to live out incarnational ministry in this moment?

I don't really know yet. If he really did lie then I probably need to confront him. If something else is going on, I'll have to figure out what to do once I know the answer to that.

23. How can I follow the leading of Christ?

I think Jesus is leading me to have a time of quiet with Him before I try to sort out this mess. I'm also sensing that even though I was upset about my host-dad's apparent dishonesty that I haven't been fully honest about something with one of my teammates. I probably need to go and confess that.

24. What action might best move me toward my highest aspiration and enhance the creative potential of this interaction, relationship, or situation?

I think at the moment it is actually to take a nap before I do anything else.

25. What, if anything, is the right thing to do? To say? To whom? How?

1. Talk to my teammate about the lie I told them.

2. Ask one of the hosts about the event that happened.

3. Go from there.

The CMD is Adapted from:
Making a World of Difference. Personal Leadership: A Methodology of Two Principles and Six Practices by Barbara, F. Schaetti, Sheila, J. Ramsey, and Gordon, C. Watanabe, 2008.

The Critical Moment responses are original.

WHAT DO YOU THINK?

What did you notice in this Critical Moment Dialogue?

If you noticed, even by the end of the CMD the author did not have all of the answers to the issue that he faced. However, he had some concrete next steps to take. Why is it important to be able to move forward in a cross-cultural relationship before or possibly even without getting all of the answers figured out?

What explanations can you think of for why the host dad did what he did? Be creative and use the frameworks from Unit 2 to think of a couple of potential explanations.

How might Personal Leadership be helpful for you in your professional practice?

TOPIC TEN: SEEING MORE THAN YOU SEE

The world presents to our senses more than we can possibly interpret. Think about what is around you at this moment – on the physical level alone there are innumerable sounds and feelings (both internal and external), textures, shades of light, smells, and even tastes. The sheer quantity of sensory input would be overwhelming if we did not select which phenomena were important and which could be ignored. Yet each of these small decisions about what to pay attention to is culturally informed. We, along with other member of our culture, give attention to some stimuli while ignoring others. For example, if you are in a classroom and look carefully around you, you may notice that there are imperfections or damage to the furniture, walls, and flooring. While you may have noticed some of those imperfections, few people are really aware of them until we look for them. It is not until we see those markings that they become noticed, which causes them to be "**figure**" in our experience of the world. Until that moment, even though they were already present, we were not experiencing them – they were background.

This situation, in which some things are called to attention and others are left unnoticed is called **figure / ground distinction**. Everything is ground (as in *background*) until we notice it.

BIG IDEA #34: COLLECT AND ANALYZE SITUATIONAL DATA FOR LATER EVALUATION

When interacting across cultures, there are times that you will need information that you are not conditioned to move from ground to figure. At the same time, there are certain cultural distractors that you may place special emphasis on that are better left as ground in those situations. For example, if you think back to the story of Elizabeth, the smell of urine was a big distractor. In Elizabeth's culture that smell may have carried significant information relating to the ability of a person to keep house. However, it is possible that for her client's family the smell was background, and carried no real significance. It could be unfortunate to let figure distinctions such as this (or roaches, condition of walls, etc.) to form the basis for life-altering action.

Yet, it is often impossible in the moment to make appropriate figure-ground distinctions in an unfamiliar culture. Fortunately, there is a way forward: jotting. **Jotting** is a way to record a large amount of information quickly, and jots form the basis of **fieldnotes**. Fieldnotes are a way to record important details regardless of the *apparent* importance of those details.

As discussed in **Topic Nine**, it is impossible to remove oneself from a situation, and it is instead necessary to take ownership of one's own involvement with the situation. The use of jotting and fieldnotes is an important step toward taking ownership.

ACTIVITY 3.6 | LEARNING TO JOT

You can practice jotting right where you are!

Use short descriptive words that you can use as shortcuts to remember what it is like to be in the situation. Along with recording the obvious "figure" elements of the situation, one of the additional goals is to bring as many elements of "ground" into "figure" as possible so that you can put yourself back in the moment later. A list of short phrases is best – don't waste time on sentences. Spend five minutes jotting down as many details as you can. Remember to include all five senses plus your internal reality. The sense of intuition is also a valid source of information for this process. Try to keep everything within this space:

Now go out into a public place and jot again. Try to go a place where you can also observe people's interactions.

The next step is to turn those jots into fieldnotes. Fieldnotes take advantage of the rich descriptive detail available in the jots and create a sensory-rich description of the environment. If you were to give the fieldnotes to a person who was not there, he or she should be able to imagine the situation as though they were there because of the level of detail available in the fieldnotes. You can choose to focus on **situational, interactional, behavioral, or other factors**, but the goal is to **put your reader into the situation.**

The reason this is important is that there may be data that you do not know is important during your first weeks of interacting with another culture. Detailed fieldnotes allow you to go back and see patterns that you were unaware of during your initial interactions – whether those are related to your own distractors or to a feature of the culture you are learning about.

ACTIVITY 3.7 | WRITING FIELDNOTES

Pick one of your sets of jottings (preferably one that has interactional or behavioral data) and practice turning it into a set of descriptive fieldnotes. The notes should come across as narrative.

Now, have someone read your fieldnotes and ask them to describe the situation to you. What details did you miss? What did you communicate that you didn't intend to?

TOPIC ELEVEN: TRANSITION

 **Discover More!**

It is important to understand the idea of cross-cultural transition if you are moving into a cross-cultural setting or working with others who are undergoing transitional experiences.

 Read *Transitions Across Cultures* from The Practical Interculturalist® and then reflect on the book below.

WHAT DO YOU THINK?

What cultural transitions have you recently experienced?

What endings have you encountered?

What beginnings have taken shape?

Describe your experience of culture shock:

SUMMARY

CULTURE MAKING | 4

Culture, as we have considered in previous units, is a social, adaptive, human response to the realities of life in a complex world. Although there are certain foundational **a priori** truths, most of how we see the world and interact with those truths is culturally constructed. This is both good and bad news. On the one hand, it means that some of the things that we may have thought were beyond question are in fact up for discussion – a reality that people with conservative commitments can be very uncomfortable with.

On the other hand, the reality that so much of our experience of reality is culturally constructed can be good news because means that we have a role in shaping it and can actively reshape it.

As Switchfoot sings:

> Is this the world you want? Is this the world you want? You're making it.
> - Switchfoot

This reality, while potentially disturbing, is also incredibly freeing. In this unit, you will consider two perspectives on culture making. The first, in **Topic Thirteen**, is a very practical theory related to the facilitation of intergroup contact.

Topic Fourteen delves further into the question of the relative malleability of culture, including ways in which you can actively look to change culture.

Finally, **Topic Fifteen** considers the topics of System, Context, and Reforming Culture, considering your role as a change agent in culture.

TOPIC THIRTEEN: CONTACT HYPOTHESIS

Many people assume that the simple act of bringing together people from different cultures will automatically result in reduced prejudice between the groups. Unfortunately, the reality is more complicated. Although increased contact between group members can **reduce prejudice**, it can also **increase prejudice**.

Fortunately, the Intergroup Contact Hypothesis can help us to understand which factors help contact between groups result in reduced prejudice between them. This is particularly important if you are 1) facilitating a situation such as a bible study, residence hall, youth program, workplace, or other social setting with participants from multiple ethnicities, or 2) you are involved with mentoring or advocating on behalf of a person who is involved in intergroup contact situations that seem to be resulting in increased prejudice.

What benefits are there to actively reducing prejudice?

BIG IDEA #35: INTERGROUP CONTACT HYPOTHESIS

Allport (1954) originally brought attention to four conditions required to facilitate reduced prejudice in intergroup contact situations. They are:

✱ Shared goals

✱ Intergroup cooperation

✱ A supporting authority

✱ Equal group status within the situation

Reviewing the research, Pettigrew (1998) added one more important factor:

✱ Friendship potential

To learn more check out this article: Pettigrew TF. (1998). Intergroup contact theory. Annual Review of Psychology, 49, 65–85.

Shared goals help to decrease prejudice between groups. Sometimes it can be difficult to find common goals between different groups. So, one of the important roles that you have is to help members of different groups to see what goals they actually share. This is really powerful when people from one group can see how they need members of another group in order to accomplish their goal.

Intergroup cooperation helps make healthy interactions, and those interactions help to reduce prejudice. Competition between groups can have the opposite effect, so be really careful setting members of different groups against each other as competitors, even if it is something as innocent as a game of basketball.

A supporting authority means that there is some authority figure (like you, or your supervisor, for example) that says it is a good thing for people from these different groups to interact with each other. It may be easier to facilitate this in the situations you have influence over than it is in general society. You can also tap into so-called "symbolic authorities" to promote the contact between groups. Symbolic authorities can be people like musicians, athletes, or politicians that group members identify with. Leaders of schools, civic institutions, and religious institutions can all serve as supporting authority as well.

Equal status within the situation is the hardest factor to really attain. In general, a policy of "we treat everyone the same" is a minimization-level response that maintains any inequalities found in society. As someone bringing together people from different groups, you have to be really careful to create *actual* equal group status within the situation that you have influence over.

Friendship potential is the most powerful of the five conditions, because it provides the most long-term positive contact that helps to decrease prejudice. Eventually that decreased prejudice spreads beyond the individual friends and extends to whole groups of people.

These five essential factors are also impacted by **time**. According to Pettigrew (1998), the first step in decreasing prejudice is **decategorization** – a recognition that an individual or several individuals from the other group do not actually fit the prejudices that you might have held before. In the decategorization stage, it would be possible, for example, for a white man to have a black friend while remaining quite racist. At that stage, he has only decategorized his friend from the stereotypes and prejudices he holds.

Over time, though, a person begins a process called **salient categorization**. This is when the new, non-prejudiced insights about the friend are extended to the whole group. In this stage, the white man we mentioned before would begin to realize that stereotypes he had previously held about black people were inaccurate, and he would begin the process of replacing these stereotypes with more accurate generalizations.

Eventually, the contact will ideally lead to **recategorization**. In recategorization, differences between groups are still acknowledged, but now they are appreciated. People from other groups are not understood as being part of the same group as you (i.e. Nebraskan, American, human). For our white friend, this might involve appreciating the contributions of both white and black groups in his church – noting the uniqueness of both groups, but understanding that they are all part of the church.

There are two other complicating factors. What happens in society in general is not something that you can control as you bring people from different groups together. At the same time, you also cannot control the experiences or personality traits that people you work with bring into the situation. These uncontrollable factors can either make it easier or harder to decrease prejudice, but you should not try to control them. Instead, acknowledge these factors as helping or challenging you so that you can focus on what you can control.

125

WHAT DO YOU THINK?

Have you ever been in an intergroup contact situation where prejudice was noticeably increased or decreased?

What happened?

How might you be able to facilitate high-quality intergroup contact situations?

AT THE INTERSECTION

Jack founded his own startup company with a group of college friends that were from several different ethnic backgrounds. The company was doing very well and Jack was invited to go on air with a deejay from the local radio station. One of the interview questions asked by the deejay was how Jack was able to be successful with his startup company in such a short time. Jack pondered for a moment before answering that the best decision he had made was to start the company with some of his dearest friends from college who were around his age group. Jack recounted that in college, he shared interests with these friends and that was key in the foundation of their friendship. They had worked on class projects together and had a lot of fun working together. Furthermore, Jack's mentor was his business professor and while in college, he and his friends had met weekly with this professor to discuss the implications of starting their own company. Jack was grateful for the supportive and encouraging attitude of his professor who pushed him and his friends to set goals and schedules to achieve the goals.

TOPIC FOURTEEN: CREATING CULTURE

As mentioned in the introduction to this unit, because so much of the way in which we understand the world is cultural, this means that there can actually be great freedom in challenging and changing the ways in which we interact with the world.

There are of course limits, and we begin there.

BIG IDEA #36: WE CAN CHANGE A LOT, BUT WE CAN'T CHANGE EVERYTHING

There are three main **things that we cannot change**. First, there are certain **a priori** truths that remain constant. As believers, we know that truth is ultimately a person – God. We also know that Truth has revealed Himself in human history through creation (Romans 1), to a people (Genesis 12). Eventually **Truth revealed Himself** in humanity through Jesus (John 1:1). Moreover we know that that although there is much we do not know about Truth, there are certain things that Truth has told us about Himself. For example in John 14:6, Truth told us that He was the way, the truth, and the life, and that no one comes to the Father except through him. So, **although there is a lot that is up for grabs in the truth market, the exclusivity of Christ is not one of them**.

The other two things that we cannot change lie at opposite ends of the size scale from each other. We cannot change "the world" and we cannot change human hearts.

Andy Crouch, in his book *Culture Making (2008)*, devotes a chapter to the idea that "we cannot change the world." Although this may seem pessimistic, Crouch's intent is to demonstrate that the world is a very large place, with something like 7 billion people in it. **To change the whole world is simply beyond our capacity.**

On the other hand, **we cannot change the hearts of our fellow humans**. We can serve as mentors, reminders, witnesses, friends, coaches, and many more things, but ultimately the shaping of the human heart is between each individual and the Spirit of God.

BIG IDEA #37: YOU CAN TAKE AN ACTIVE APPROACH TO SHAPING CULTURE

Many Christians have roles that are particularly connected to working with people who are in some way **marginalized**. For example, if you work with youth who are in foster care, juvenile justice or for some other reason have one or more case workers, we can refer to these youth as being 'in the system'. To be a youth 'in the system' is to, by definition, be marginalized from so-called 'normal' society. The space you occupy alongside marginalized people is one of the most **exciting places to see new forms of culture arise**. People who are marginalized are less committed to the way things are, and are often looking for new solutions to very real problems.

If you work with marginalized people, then your role is especially valid in this regard because people are best able to shape culture in areas over which they have significant authority. While you likely will not be able to change "the system" in substantive ways (at least not initially, and certainly not alone), most of us have **micro-cultural environments in which we exercise authority**. In those environments, you may have the freedom to take an active approach to rewriting certain cultural narratives and scripts.

There are some cultural 'purists' who insist that changing culture is an imperialistic endeavor. While that certainly can be the case, changing culture can also be a good form of engagement. Kwame Appiah argues in his 2006 article "The Case for Contamination" that cultural change is a constant feature of all cultures, and that it would be inappropriate to keep from changing culture based on some supposed 'pure' cultural form that we might disrupt. Instead, it is better to take an active role in shaping culture for human flourishing. Remember, culture can be **adaptive** or **maladaptive**, and is always a mixture of these two. It may thus be entirely appropriate to root out the maladaptive traits and narratives and to supplant them with adaptive traits and narratives.

In the cultural change process, you will at times encounter deep **resistance**. Such resistance may not be spoken or even articulated. This is not surprising in that much resistance to change is rooted in the deep values level of cultures – the levels which are often not known even to people within the culture (remember the fish and the water?). Thus, people may argue against the kinds of changes you wish to make without a clear idea of why they oppose you. You can use **deep cultural analysis** to help any opponents discover their root concerns and work toward mutually beneficial solutions.

ACTIVITY 4.1 | CREATING CULTURE IN YOUR CONTEXT

Imagine that you have the opportunity to significantly reshape your primary context – whether that is a residence hall, a workplace, a youth group, a classroom, etc. Your task is to create the best possible culture for the success of the people who are part of this context. Let's walk through a process of creating culture.

Identify Values:

1. **Organization values:** Think about the larger organization that your context exists within. Or, if you are an entrepreneur, think about your company. What does your organization believe is really important? These may be stated values, but often they are even deeper than what is stated. For example, one organization has stated that it exists to affect youth with the life-changing message of Jesus Christ, releasing them to be who God intends them to be. This is true, but it is even more deeply true that that organization values discipleship of both its clients and its staff. Important decisions are made every day on this value of discipleship, even if it isn't specifically named. What values does the organization have that should underlay the culture of your workplace?

2. **Personal Values:** What values do you bring into the situation? These may overlap or be different from the organization values.

3. **System Values:** What values are held by the larger system in which you function? These can include government agencies, accrediting bodies, and so on.

4. **Participant Values:** What values do your employees, customers, residents, etc. bring into the situation?

5. **Values Analysis:** Of the values you have identified, which ones overlap? Which ones conflict?

Beliefs: For each of the groups above, which beliefs (about the self, organization, system, etc.) have developed to sustain the values and translate them into behaviors? For example, if a resident or a student values self-protection, he might develop a belief of personal worthlessness so as to avoid disappointing himself.

1. Organization Beliefs:

2. Personal Beliefs:

3. System Beliefs:

4. Participant Beliefs:

5. **Beliefs Analysis:** Which of the above beliefs will aid you in translating desired values into behaviors? Which will cause trouble for you? How do the various beliefs interact with each other?

Identify Outcomes:

1. Participant outcomes: Make a list of your ideal outcomes for the youth who will participate in your context.

2. Your outcomes: Make a list of your ideal outcomes for your context and for yourself.

Identify Assets:

1. **Participant Assets:** What strengths and resources do the customers, residents, employees, etc. bring to the home?

2. **Societal assets:** What strengths and resources does society provide for the success of you and the participants?

3. **Your Assets:** What strengths and resources do you and the organization bring to the context?

Identify Cultural Pre-conditioning: What cultural values, beliefs, and behaviors are already present?

1. Society (majority culture)

2. Participants' culture

3. System culture (accreditors, government, etc,)

4. Organizational culture

5. Your Culture

Design a culture: Knowing what you know about your desired outcomes, the assets you have to work with, and the cultural preconditioning present, how do you want your workplace to function? For example, if you are an RA and want your residence hall to instill self-worth through identity formation, and you think a family atmosphere is an important way to make that happen, describe how it would happen.

Cultural SUBVERSION: What elements of preexisting culture will you need to actively subvert in order to be successful? How will you do this?

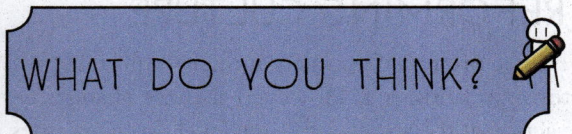

WHAT DO YOU THINK?

One of the key points of this section is that even though culture is deep and significant, you can – at least to a certain extent – create and change culture. Having gone through this activity, what you have you learned about why it is hard to create and change culture?

Why is cultural self-awareness necessary to begin a cultural change project?

As you went through the activity, did you gain any insights about potential strengths already present – strengths brought by the organization, yourself, the system, or the participant?

At this point, do you feel like culture-making and cultural change are attainable? Why or why not?

The process that you just went through worked its way up the cultural iceberg, starting with values and beliefs and moving toward behaviors. Did you find that process to be helpful? Why or why not?

TOPIC FIFTEEN: SYSTEM, CONTEXT, AND REFORMING CULTURE

As mentioned in the previous topic, it is possible to engage in major cultural change projects if you start at micro-cultural levels, such as within a bible study, small workplace environment, or even a mentoring relationship. However, if those changes are ultimately to be effective in society, it is necessary to also understand and take action at the societal-cultural level. In many cases, this will be at the local (city/county) and state levels. Although national action is appropriate in some cases, it is also the most difficult and can often be less effective in promoting attitudinal changes in the short run.

What do you think the roles of systems, context, and cultural patterns are in forming individual decisions and expressions? How can you assess the blend between internal and external responsibility?

SUMMARY

BIBLICAL AND THEOLOGICAL REFLECTIONS | 5

Millennials today occupy a difficult space in contemporary Christianity. Conservative evangelical Christianity has over the last 120 years largely **failed to effectively engage the societal challenges** faced by the poor and marginalized, such as those that many Millennials desire to serve effectively. This has left churches, businesses, and even social-service agencies uncertain of how to interact with socially minded Christian Millennials.

The goal of this short unit is to provide a few foundational biblical and theological reflections on which to base the socially minded, Jesus-centered work at the organizational and individual level. There are of course whole theological visions that have been written toward this end, so the aim in this unit is not to be comprehensive. Instead, the goal is to prompt theological reflection for you in your own context.

To do this, we will engage a few topics of primary importance:

* The Gospel: Truth and truth
* Missiological presence
* Biblical engagement with society
* Partnerships
* Reliance on the Spirit

TOPIC SIXTEEN: THE GOSPEL - TRUTH AND TRUTH

The Gospel is the most important message of Christianity. Yet when I have asked believers to define the Gospel, I find that many are unable to do so. Some sheepishly suggest that the Gospel is the books of Matthew, Mark, Luke, and John in the Bible. While it is true that those books are referred to as the "Gospels", what we are looking for is the central truth of our faith. It is important, then to begin this section by wrestling with how we define the Gospel.

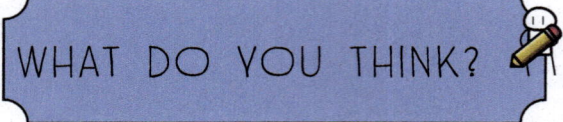

Before going any further, stop and define the Gospel in the way in which you are most familiar / comfortable:

Now, having done that, let us proceed to a detailed exploration of the Gospel.

ACTIVITY 5.1 | THE THIN AND THICK GOSPEL

In this activity, you will walk through a series of questions designed to clarify what the Gospel is. It is recommended that you have a bible handy.

At its core, what is the Gospel? That is to say, what is the irreducible message of Christianity? Think of it this way: If you subtract anything from this core, it is no longer the Gospel.

What is the mechanism *of the Gospel? That is, how does the Gospel work?*

What is the motive *for the Gospel? This is the question of why. Why did God do what he did to make the Gospel available to people? What is the goal of the Gospel?*

What are the individual effects *of the Gospel? What changes for/in/about a person who receives the Gospel?*

What are the community effects *of the Gospel? What changes in relationships when people receive the Gospel?*

Look through the New Testament for statements that include a phrase like "you once were" or "you now are." Example: 1 Peter 2:10 (CEV) "Once you were nobody. Now you are God's people. At one time no one had pity on you. Now God has treated you with kindness." Make a list of these verses.

According to the verses you found, what are the effects of the Gospel?

Return now to your original definition of the Gospel and the core of the Gospel that you identified. There may be a difference between what you listed in the original definition and some of the elements of the Gospel you have found through further reflection. This difference, when it exists, can be considered the difference between the *thin* Gospel and the *thick* Gospel. Both are true versions of the Gospel, but they have different aims. The *thin* Gospel aims to help people know how they can be reconciled to God through Jesus Christ through the forgiveness of sins. The *thick* Gospel explains how people who have been reconciled to God begin to live differently in the world, and how this changes not only their own lives, but also the lives of people around them. The thick Gospel is not true without the thin Gospel. At the same time, the thin Gospel introduces people to Jesus Christ, who will move them toward the thick Gospel.

Have you thought of the Gospel in terms of thin and thick before? What do you like about this? What makes you uncomfortable about it?

BIG IDEA #38: TRUTH HAS REVEALED HIMSELF

As discussed in the previous unit, there is truth which supersedes all other truths. Remember, as believers, we know that truth is ultimately a person – the three-in-one God. We also know that Truth has revealed Himself in human history through creation (Romans 1), and to a people (Genesis 12). Eventually **Truth revealed Himself** in humanity through Jesus (John 1:1).

We know that that although there is much we do not know about Truth, there are certain things that Truth has told us about Himself. For example in John 14:6, Truth told us that He was the way, the truth, and the life, and that no one comes to the Father except through him. So, again, **although there is a lot that is up for grabs in the truth market, the exclusivity of Christ is not one of them.**

 **Discover More!**

Read more:

Social Constructivism & Christianity: A Disturbingly Short Guide to Everything by Stephen W. Jones.

One of the limitations that American Christians often face in the discussion of intercultural competence relates to the difficulty of understanding other perspectives as valid. We fear that if we acknowledge the validity of other perspectives that all truth becomes relative, that we no longer have the right to the exclusive truth claim the Gospel requires. However, this is simply not the case. In recognizing the validity of other perspectives, we recognize the limitations of every human in grasping the fullness of truth. All of us have some of it right and all of us have some of it wrong. This does not in any way endanger the existence of truth.

Rather, the acknowledgement that we have only an imperfect understanding of the perfect, and a finite understanding of the infinite, frees us up to be much more intellectually honest. It removes God from our small boxes.

The Gospel is available for people from every culture. In God's kingdom, there is no people favored to receive the Gospel above any other – Jesus clearly emphasized that the Gospel was for Jerusalem, Judea, Samaria, and to the ends of the earth (Acts 1:8),

The Gospel necessarily stands in critique of every culture, including ours. Jesus said that in all nations people must be taught to do the things he commanded as they become his disciples (Mt 28:19-20).

BIG IDEA #39: THE GOSPEL SPEAKS TO DEEP VALUES IN ALL CULTURES

The cornerstone of the Christian faith is the Gospel of Jesus Christ: Humanity has been separated from a right relationship with God and each other because of sin, and only Jesus can set that right through his death on the cross and resurrection. Ultimately, because of Jesus's death and resurrection, evil and death will lose, and all will be set right by God in His time. In the meantime, people who are reconciled to God and each other through Jesus live as members of the church and have the indwelling power and presence of His Spirit.

The Gospel can be communicated in many different ways that are equally valid, but all contain the central element of Jesus, and Him crucified. Recall the discussion in Unit 2 about three primary human motivations: Guilt/Innocence, Shame/Honor, Fear/Power. The Gospel speaks equally well to all three of these.

Majority culture American Christians will likely be most familiar with the Guilt/Innocence presentation of the Gospel, with a strong emphasis on the book of Romans: You have **sinned** and fallen short of the glory of God, have earned **death**, and you cannot make yourself innocent. Jesus, as the only sinless human, was the only one who could pay your debt and **give you innocence** (propitiation). He paid the cost for all people at the Cross, and because he rose from the dead, we know that the debt is paid. All you have to do to receive forgiveness of sins is to receive it – the innocence you lack is provided by Jesus, and God will see you as righteous because of Him.

Christians from Shame/Honor cultures may emphasize the story of the Prodigal Son, who had **shamed** his family terribly and (depending on the culture) the only ways to restore honor were **disowning, suicide, or being killed by his family.** Instead, the Father **embraces** the son and restores him to **honor.** Again, this perspective of the Gospel is accomplished through the work of Christ, who is the firstborn among many brethren (Romans 8:29). This language of adoption is particularly important, as is the recognition that when the Accuser stands against us, it is Christ himself who mediates on our behalf.

Christians from a Fear/Power perspective may emphasize Jesus' miracles and ultimately his **victory over death.** As believers, we are able to enter into that **Power** through the Holy Spirit, by which we are sealed for the day of redemption. Verses such as Luke 10:19, Matthew 16:18, John 4:4, 1 John 4:18, and Romans 8:38–39 may be particularly important from this perspective, especially in reaffirming that the **powers of darkness cannot have victory** over the believer.

In each case, Jesus is the critical answer to a human problem. In each case as well, the deepest human problem is estrangement from God, which has caused guilt, shame, and fear. God restores people to right relationship with Himself through Jesus' finished work on the Cross and makes it possible for us to live with Him forever through the Resurrection. There is no other Gospel other than Jesus crucified and resurrected.

The power of this Gospel is particularly important to understand in your work, as there are many people who suffer under various addictions and live under fear. Ultimately the power of the Gospel has the freedom to release individuals from those things. For some this is immediate, for others it is a long, slow, ongoing fight.

WHAT DO YOU THINK?

Which Gospel emphasis resonates the most clearly with you?

How is the Gospel communicated through your work?

TOPIC SEVENTEEN: MISSIONAL PRESENCE

In our vocations, many believers occupy an important intersection between the church and society. In this position, it is possible to have a strong and sustained witness.

One of the most important contributions that believers can make in society is to demonstrate the Character of God and to invite people into a living relationship with Him.

BIG IDEA #40: FOLLOWERS OF JESUS EXTEND HIS INVITATION TO LIVE IN HIS KINGDOM

In Matthew 4 (v. 17), as Jesus begins his ministry, we read "from that time Jesus began to preach, saying "repent, for the kingdom of heaven is at hand." Although there are various eschatological interpretations of the Kingdom, **the invitation to live with Jesus as King is still very much available**. As we receive the Gospel and our status with God is restored (Romans 5:10-11), we also enter into the authority of a different kingdom. In Philippians Paul notes that **we are citizens of Heaven**. As such we are **ambassadors** of the King, who make known His will here on earth (let Your Kingdom come, Your will be done, on earth as it is in Heaven). From this understanding, we can examine what Jesus said about the Kingdom and how it might shape the ways in which we live, think, and work.

As we extend this invitation, sharing the Gospel of Jesus there are a few points to keep in mind:

- You do not need to become like me to receive the Gospel. Consider Phillip and the Ethiopian Eunuch (Acts 8:26-40), Peter and Cornelius (Acts Chapter 10), Paul and the Gentiles (Acts 13:47-52). It has been a temptation for the church through the ages to look down on culturally different others, and to even consider some people as unworthy of the Gospel because of their behavior or background. Jesus himself demonstrated this attitude as false when he encountered the woman at the well in John 4.

- Sharing the Gospel is not the same as spreading culture. This was determined in the Jerusalem Council of Acts 15. Certain early Christians thought it was necessary to become culturally Jewish in order to partake of the Gospel. However, God both demonstrated to the church and led the Jerusalem Council to understand that this was false. As we mentioned before, the Gospel is both available to people from any culture and stands in critique of every culture. There is no "biblical culture" to which we are to aspire. Rather, we should look to live biblically within our cultures.

- Culture does not need to stop the Gospel's progress. Indeed, Romans 15:14-33 demonstrates how Paul was not only planning to further preach the Gospel (even into Spain), but how it had taken root in such widely different places as Jerusalem, Illyricum, Macedonia, and Achaia – to such an extent that Gentile believers in Macedonia and Achaia were sending gifts to Jewish believers in Jerusalem, though they were united only by Christ's Gospel and not by culture.

WHAT DO YOU THINK?

Are any of these points challenging to you? If so, how so?

How would you describe the interaction between the Gospel and culture in your work?

BIG IDEA #41 LIVING IN THE KINGDOM INVOLVES A "RADICALLY" DIFFERENT VALUE SET

The Sermon on the Mount, which closely follows Jesus' initial teaching of "repent, for the kingdom of heaven is at hand," Jesus lays out a set of values that challenge existing systems and sensibilities. To say that this system is "radically" different is to say that *at the root*, it takes a different direction. This concept is explained by Jesus and other scripture writers who over and over affirm that the system of the Kingdom is different from the system of man.

Consider, for example, what Jesus says is *blessed* (CEV):

> *God blesses those people who depend only on him.*
>
> *They belong to the kingdom of heaven! (Mt 5:3)*
>
> *God blesses those people who grieve.*
>
> *They will find comfort! (Mt 5:4)*
>
> *God blesses those people who are humble.*
>
> *The earth will belong to them! (Mt 5:5)*

God blesses those people who want to obey him more than to eat or drink.

They will be given what they want! (Mt 5:6)

God blesses those people who are merciful.

They will be treated with mercy! (Mt 5:7)

God blesses those people whose hearts are pure.

They will see him! (Mt 5:8)

God blesses those people who make peace.

They will be called his children! (Mt 5:9)

God blesses those people who are treated badly for [the sake of righteousness and justice].

They belong to the kingdom of heaven. (Mt 5:10)

God will bless you when people insult you, mistreat you, and tell all kinds of evil lies about you because of me. Be happy and excited! You will have a great reward in heaven. People did these same things to the prophets who lived long ago. (Mt 5:11-12)

The values of the Kingdom are radically different than the values of human endeavors, which emphasize strength, success, power, and outward appearances. Over and over, the values of Jesus shocked the values of the religious people of the day, as he proclaimed a Kingdom of inward righteousness and of outward justice, both of which come together in the command to "be perfect, as your heavenly Father is perfect" (Mt 5:48).

BIG IDEA #42: FOLLOWERS OF JESUS SHARE THE KINGDOM THROUGH EXCELLENCE AND GENTLENESS

In the "high priestly prayer" Jesus made on behalf of his followers before he was Crucified, Jesus specifically asked that his followers *not be* taken out of the world, in spite of the reality that we do not belong to the world. Instead, he prays that the Father would keep us from the evil one. As we interpret our role in the world, it is important to bear in mind that Jesus wanted people to come to know the Father through our witness. One of the markers that gives us hearing in the sight of the world is excellence. Consider Joseph and Daniel, who both maintained a distinctive identity in foreign lands, yet served with such **excellence** that they were highly valued by rulers who did not know God. Consider also this call from Paul:

> *Do your work willingly, as though you were serving the Lord himself, and not just your earthly master. In fact, the Lord Christ is the one you are really serving, and you know that he will reward you. (Col. 3:23-24)*

So, on the one hand we serve with excellence. Yet on the other hand, we see Jesus advocating values that seem opposed to excellence. His associates are of questionable character. He welcomes children. He opposes the externally successful and prefers to associate with those who know their brokenness. He praises the widow who gives a penny, covers the sin of an adulteress, and lifts up the actions of a compassionate foreigner in the story of the Good Samaritan. Jesus' call is not one to excellence for our own sake. Instead, it is a call to tremendous gentleness – a **gentleness** that is possible through the empowerment of the Spirit of God (it is, in fact, one of the fruit of the Spirit in Galatians 5). Moreover, Jesus himself was both gentle and humble in heart (Mt. 11:29).

We are freed to be both excellent and gentle because we do not need to provide for or advance ourselves. Our worth is settled in Christ, and we are thus freed to be open to the anonymity of loving the broken, and equally free to excel in society for the sake of the King.

BIG IDEA #43: KINGDOM VALUES UPEND TRADITIONAL NOTIONS OF GUILT, SHAME, AND FEAR

As you have already considered, three primary motivators in the human psyche are Guilt, Shame, and Fear. Each culture tends to lean toward these in different amounts.

In each case, the Gospel upends the traditional notion, which makes it necessary for us to reexamine our commitment to these notions as we live our Christian witness. For example, it is no longer sufficient to think of those with felony records as 'guilty,' and those without as 'innocent.' The gospel tells us that none is innocent, and that aside from Christ none of us can become innocent.

The Gospel tells us that not only are we **guilty**, but that we are also shameful and that we should be **afraid** of God, afraid of people, afraid of creation, afraid of spiritual forces, and afraid of ourselves. An honest assessment of the human condition as understood by the Gospel is tragic indeed.

It is important to recognize that this does not apply only to those who are imprisoned, to those who are poor, those who are marginalized. This reality applies equally to all people. There is none who is righteous, and even our righteousness is like filthy rags to God. This gospel reality must upend our sense of superiority and judgment when working with "returning citizens" leaving prison and our incarcerated brothers and sisters. **You are not better than the people you help. Not at all.** It is only by God's grace that you are able to help others at all.

BIG IDEA #44: KINGDOM VALUES UPEND OUR NOTIONS OF INNOCENCE, HONOR, AND POWER

At the same time that the Gospel frees us to acknowledge our brokenness alongside all other people, it also disrupts the ways in which we (falsely) attempt to solve the problems of guilt, shame, and fear. Jesus deeply opposed the ways by which we attempt to accord honor, innocence, and power to ourselves through self-righteous religious practices and marginalizing social distinctions.

Paul (who rebuked Peter, if your recall), and James are particularly clear on this point. Our former social distinctions are put aside. There is no Jew, no Greek, no Male, no Female. We are one in Christ. Similarly, favoritism must not be shown to those with power or wealth. Because society is built to reinforce these ideas, we must actively push against them.

Followers of Jesus must upend the unhealthy pursuit of honor and esteem outside of Christ through loving the marginalized of society, bringing them into the family, and challenging the self-righteous to acknowledge their own brokenness.

WHAT DO YOU THINK?

How do you understand the missional presence that you have in the community as a follower of Jesus?

How do you demonstrate the values of the Kingdom individually and together with other Jesus-followers?

Which is harder for you to pursue: excellence or gentleness?

Are any of the theological ideas presented in this section challenging to you? Which ones? Why?

TOPIC EIGHTEEN: CHRISTIAN ENGAGEMENT WITH SOCIETY

Throughout time and space, Christians have interpreted the role of Christians in Society from widely different viewpoints.

This brief section cannot satisfactorily introduce you to the many models that have been suggested for navigating the tensions surrounding living out the Gospel in society. If this topic is particularly interesting to you, check out the additional reading below.

Discover More!

Read more!

 *Center Church by Tim Keller (2012)*

 *The Gospel in Pluralist Society by Lesslie Newbigin (1989)*

 *Christ and Culture by H. Richard Neihbuhr (2001)*

BIG IDEA #45:   SHARING THE GOSPEL, AT ITS BEST, INVOLVES BOTH LIVING AND VERBAL PROCLAMATION

The American church experienced a significant schism in the late nineteenth century. Sometimes called *The Great Reversal*, the division related to whether the Gospel was spiritual or social in nature. One half decided that the Gospel was social, and that the church's most important work was institutional in nature. The other half decided that the Gospel was spiritual and that the church's most important work was the spiritual salvation of individuals. Regarding another schism, Paul asked in 1 Corinthians a question relevant for us today (ESV):

Is Christ divided?

For most of church history, the assumption was that the Gospel had both individual salvific power as well as an impact on society. Gospel ministry, at its best, involved both living and verbal proclamation. If other Christians challenge you on the legitimacy of the elements of your ministry that are not specifically evangelistic, their position comes from this divide. The proponents of the spiritual-only response rejected most forms of collective engagement (up until the rise of the moral majority). On the other hand, if a Christian encourages you in the great social work that you do but does not approve of your involvement in bringing others to faith in Christ (i.e., evangelism), this too comes from the Great Reversal.

James and the Epistles of John (First, Second, and Third John) make it abundantly clear that true religion does involve meeting felt needs as well as sharing the news that Jesus is the King who offers salvation.

Faith without works is dead, and works without faith are dead.

BIG IDEA #46: WE DEMONSTRATE THE KINGDOM THROUGH THE WITNESS OF THE MULTIETHNIC CHURCH

One of the strongest witnesses of the power of the Gospel is sustained fellowship between believers of different socioeconomic, ethnic, and national backgrounds. This was an issue of particular importance in the New Testament church, and it played out in the tension between Jews and Gentiles. Specifically at issue was whether it was necessary for Gentiles to become like Jews in order to become Christians. It was decided in the Jerusalem Council of Acts 15 that it was not necessary to become culturally Jewish in order to be Christian. Instead, the Council wrote to the non-Jewish believers with these words (excerpts from Acts 15:28-29):

The Holy Spirit has shown us that we should not place any extra burden on you. But you should not eat anything offered to idols. [...] You must also not commit any terrible sexual sins. If you follow these instructions, you will do well. We send our best wishes.

Perhaps one of the most beautiful realities of the Gospel is that the people who know Christ are brought into **the church**, which is a **multi-national** (Acts 2), **multi-ethnic** (Galatians 3), **people group** (1 Peter 2) with different **socioeconomic classes** (1 Corinthians 11, James 2, Philemon), **gifting**, and **roles** (Romans 12, 1 Corinthians 12, Ephesians 4).

The unity available to believers through the Gospel is not restricted to unity within a particular culture, but is rather intended for the church as a whole (John 17, Romans 12, 1 Corinthians 12) and is a testimony to all. Even in the eschatalogical vision of John in Revelation, there continue to be nations (Revelation 22), and all cultures are represented among this beautiful picture (Revelation 7:9-17, emphasis added):

After this, I saw a large crowd with more people than could be counted. They were from every race, tribe, nation, and language, and they stood before the throne and before the Lamb. They wore white robes and held palm branches in their hands, as they shouted,

"Our God, who sits upon the throne, has the power to save his people, and so does the Lamb."

The angels who stood around the throne knelt in front of it with their faces to the ground. The elders and the four living creatures knelt there with them. Then they all worshiped God and said,

"Amen! Praise, glory, wisdom, thanks, honor, power, and strength belong to our God forever and ever! Amen!"

One of the elders asked me, "Do you know who these people are that are dressed in white robes? Do you know where they come from?"

"Sir," I answered, "you must know."

Then he told me: "These are the ones who have gone through the great suffering. They have washed their robes in the blood of the Lamb and have made them white. And so they stand before the throne of God and worship him in his temple day and night. The one who sits on the throne will spread his tent over them. They will never hunger or thirst again, and they won't be troubled by the sun or any scorching heat.

The Lamb in the center of the throne will be their shepherd. He will lead them to streams of life-giving water, and God will wipe all tears from their eyes."

Finally, we see that as believers we are instructed to have special concern for other believers, our brothers and sisters (Philippians 2:1-4, emphasis added):

Christ encourages you, and his love comforts you. God's Spirit unites you, and you are concerned for others. Now make me completely happy! Live in harmony by showing love for each other. Be united in what you think, as if you were only one person. Don't be jealous or proud, but be humble and consider others more important than yourselves. Care about them as much as you care about yourselves.

If you apply this last idea to our relationships with believers from various cultures, it should become obvious that our love for one another as believers, especially from different backgrounds, stands as one of the most unique and beautiful representations of the Gospel. We are freed to be earnestly concerned with the trials and difficulties faced by our Christian brothers and sisters, and it is not necessary for them to become culturally like us in order for us to enter into fellowship!

TOPIC NINETEEN: PARTNERSHIPS

BIG IDEA #47: NOT ALL THEOLOGIES ARE CREATED EQUAL (OR: MAKE THE MAIN THINGS THE MAIN THINGS)

When looking to partner with others in ministry, it can be difficult to know where to draw lines of distinction and where to emphasize unity. It can be tempting to draw lines of distinction where they do not belong, and the following activity may help you consider which lines are appropriate and which are not.

ACTIVITY 5.2 | THEOLOGICAL PRIORITIES

Imagine that theology can be divided into three different tiers.

The **first tier** contains the highest priority of theological ideas. These are essential in understanding salvation. An example is that Jesus is the Son of God.

The **second tier** contains important issues, but ones which are not essential to salvation. An example could be the roles of women and men in ministry, or the role of the spiritual gifts.

The **third tier** contains times of preference. An example could be choices related to style of worship, types of youth ministry or service activities, or even the color of the carpet. Sadly, many churches that split do so over tier three issues.

Theologians think there about 5–7 tier one items. There are innumerable tier two and tier three items. Attempt to identify at least 5 items in each category:

TIER 1:	TIER 2:	TIER 3
✳	✳	✳
✳	✳	✳
✳	✳	✳
✳	✳	✳
✳	✳	✳

One of the interesting things to do with this activity is to share your tier one items with friends and coworkers. It is surprising how often even believers of the same nationality, ethnicity, denomination, age, and gender will place different items into tier one. The point is not that there are no tier one issues, but that we should be cautious about who we exclude from partnership because of theological differences. It may be useful for you to seek out a common "core of the Gospel" with other Jesus-followers that you work and minister with. You can then emphasize these truths above other, less important theological concepts.

BIG IDEA #48: WORKING WITH "THE WORLD"

It is necessary for Jesus-followers to partner with "the world" system. We do this as we work with federal, state, and local government; through work with nongovernmental agencies and non-profits; and generally through the corporate and finance sectors. It is necessary to engage these systems as we minister among hurting, broken, and marginalized people that we come into contact with.

Read Philippians 4:4-8; and all of 1 Peter.

What practical advice does Peter give to Christians about living out the Gospel?

In what ways does gentleness differentiate you as you live in the world?

What about the way in which these passages say to live would make people want you to explain your faith?

TOPIC TWENTY: RELIANCE ON THE SPIRIT

BIG IDEA #49: THE SPIRIT OF GOD IS STILL AROUND

The role of the Holy Spirit in the life of the believer is a complicated and contested issue. But while there are many different interpretations of the role of the Spirit, here are a few considerations you can rely on:

1. The Spirit of God lives in believers, seals them for salvation, and protects them from evil.

2. Believers can live with a growing sensitivity to the Spirit, or can quench His voice.

3. Life with the Holy Spirit empowers believers to demonstrate love, joy, peace, patience, kindness, gentleness, and self-control (Gal. 5).

4. There are spiritual enemies, but the Spirit of God is more powerful than those, and that power is accessible to believers.

5. The Holy Spirit is also active in the lives of people who don't know Christ, and will sometimes be in the process of drawing such people to Him, preparing them to hear and respond to the Gospel.

AT THE INTERSECTION

John is a jazz musician from Malaysia. In 2011, he had an encounter with God that changed his life while on tour in China. When he returned to Malaysia, he began using his gigs as a platform to share the gospel with his audiences. He also had many opportunities to share his passion for music and for God with other musicians. Many who came into contact with John were blessed by his genuine love for them. One night, in between sets at a jazz lounge, he sat down with four young adults who turned out to be tourists from Eastern Europe. As they spoke, one of the young men opened up and shared with John some of anxiety he was facing. John prayed for this young man and he experienced an incredible supernatural peace and gave his life to Jesus right there at the bar.

John began taking this ministry to the streets. He prayed for people he met on the street who were in wheelchairs and crutches and saw many cases of instantaneous healing. John invited some of his like-minded friends to go out on the streets to pray for the sick with him. They saw many miracles happen and they began inviting more people to join them on their ministry team. Within a couple of months, the group grew from just a few people to over fifty.

John continues his ministry on Monday nights with a group of passionate people who hit the streets to pray for the sick and share the transforming power of the gospel with people who have not yet experienced the love of God. Through John and his friends, God has opened blind eyes, healed the lame, and delivered those under spiritual bondage. John has no intentions of drawing attention upon himself, but credits all healing power to the Holy Spirit. "There are no superstar Christians," John will say, "just ones that are willing to be obedient in following the leading of the Holy Spirit. God is still doing miracles in this day and age!"

AT THE INTERSECTION

Ravi is a minister in India. He travels from village to village, preaching the gospel and praying for the sick. Ravi has seen an incredible amount of people get healed and delivered from spiritual bondage. A documentary team from California heard about Ravi's ministry and traveled to India to interview Ravi on how he conducts his ministry. Ravi sat down with the team and shared with them how he operates. Early every morning, Ravi wakes up and prays. He asks God very specific questions concerning the day's agenda. After several hours of praying and listening, Ravi begins his day by carrying out each and everything he heard from God in his time of prayer.

One day, God woke Ravi up at 4am and told him that he was to go up a mountain and into a village that has a water pump next to a bridge. Ravi woke the entire team up and they set out for this village. After several hours of walking, they saw a bridge and a water pump next to it. Ravi entered the village and begins preaching the gospel as people gather around him to listen. In the midst of his preaching, a crowd of men yielding long knives walk into the village. Ravi did not waver and continued preaching the gospel. When he finished, he asked the people whether anyone would want to know Jesus as their own God. A man raised his hand and stepped forward. Ravi prayed with the man to accept Christ into his life and afterwards the man expresses that he feels an incredible amount of peace descend upon his being.

It was then that Ravi and the team discovered that this man was the religious patriarch who plays host to the largest religious celebration in the region. He and his men had heard that Ravi was preaching at one of his villages and had come to stop Ravi. Instead, he encountered the transforming power of the gospel. On that day itself, he began telling his followers to trust in Jesus as their Lord and Savior.

Discover More!

For more, check out *Life in the Spirit* by A.W. Tozer (2009)

SUMMARY

Key Ideas

Activities

GLOSSARY

a priori Before, prior to, already.

adapt Making adjustments in the way a person or group solves the basic questions of life based on external forces.

adaptive Adaptations to environmental (social, geographical, political, etc) factors that ultimately help sustain the success of the group.

agency Refers to the ability of a person to take control of their own situation.

baggage Elements that are external to a relationship or situation yet have an impact on that relationship or situation. People often bring these elements in without knowing they are doing so.

beliefs Strongly held ideas. These are often specific, and sometimes codified. People are much more aware of their own beliefs than their values.

bonding relationships In-group ties that help to affirm identity an provide access to within-group resources.

bridging relationships Ties that cross group boundaries and provide access to external resources.

collectivism A cultural pattern for answering the identity question. Collectivism suggests that identity is primarily with the group and only secondarily (if at all) as an individual.

conflict styles These are the combinations of direct/indirect and emotionally expressive/restrained communication styles. There are four posibilities: direct & restrained; direct & expressive; indirect & restrained; indirect & expressive.

continuum Use with frameworks, where there are two main patterns, but any specific culture may be any combination of two patterns. For example, in identity the two patterns are individualism and collectivism, but a person or culture could be anywhere from very individualistic to slightly individualistic to slightly collectivistic to extremely collectivistic, or anywhere in between.

creativity In the Personal Leadership context, refers to the process of *creating* one's responses to complex cross-cultural situations, bringing multiple insights and perspectives to bear.

crisis orientation An approach to planning that emphasizes all possible eventualities and attempts to control for them.

culture How people do their stuff together. Milton Bennett also defines culture as the learned and shared values, beliefs, and behaviors of a group of interacting people.

decategorization A first step in prejudice reduction, where prior categories are recognized as being overly simplistic and innaccurate.

direct communication A way to convey meaning that encodes the message primarily into the words that are spoken.

emotional expression A communication pattern in which respect is earned and shared through externalizing emotion rather than internalizing it.

emotional restraint A communication pattern in which respect is earned and shared through internalizing emotion rather than expressing it.

enculturation The process of growing up in a culture and taking on the values and norms of that culture.

ethnographic skills Are useful for studying cultural patterns, especially among an unfamiliar group.

ethnography An in depth study of the cultural patterns of a particular group.

fieldnotes Renderings of jottings that enable other people to enter the situation the author experienced. Usually rich in sensory and/or relational detail.

figure / ground distinction The process by which humans determine what stimuli are noticed and which can be ignored. This is usually subconscious.

frameworks Ways to explain general patterns of behavior and communication without stereotyping.

generalizations An alternative to stereotypes, generalizations accurately describe general tendencies within groups, and are always used tentatively as regards any individual member of a group.

hypodescent The culturally-constructed belief that any non-white heritage makes a person non-white (i.e. a White and Black parents have a Black child).

identity The complex set of factors that make up a person's self concept.

indirect communication A way to convey meaning that does not primarily code the message into the words that are spoken. The message may be conveyed through a mediator, through story, or some other non-direct means.

individualism A cultural pattern for answering the identity question. Individualism suggests that identity is primarily with the individual and only secondarily (if at all) as a member of the group.

jotting A way to record a large amount of situational and interactional information quickly.

maladaptive An adaptation to environmental (social, geographical, political, etc) factors that ultimately threatens the success of the group.

marginalized Refers to people, or groups of people, who are not able to participate fully in society's ideals due perhaps to exclusion, personal incapacity, or oppression.

mindfulness Full and intentional awareness of self and situation.

mitigate To intentionally work to reduce the ill-effects of something.

monochronic An understanding of time as a limited, linear resource.

non-crisis orientation An approach to planning that emphasizes living in the moment, and that tend toward being fatalistic about crises (i.e. "we couldn't have prevented it anyway")

particularism An approach to ethics that emphasizes the details and relationships surrounding any particular ethical question.

personal leadership A method for succesfull interactions across cultures based on mindfulness and creativity, and employing six practices. See Schaetti, Ramsey, and Watanabe's book *Personal Leadership*.

phenotype The physical look of a person (i.e. skin color, ear and nose size, hair color, etc.)

phoneme A basic unit of sound, that can distinguish one word from another.

polychronic An understanding of time as fluid, circular, abundant, and multi-channeled.

proximal host The locally-known group that a person is assumed to belong to based on external factors, such as appearance.

race A culturally constructed notion that assumes that cultural traits have biological basis.

racialized Refers to a society in which race is a primary way to identify and label people.

recategorization A late stage in prejudice reduction, in which people recognize that although group distinctions exist, there are are also significant similarities and shared humanity between groups.

reflexive skills Enable a person to become fully aware of the way(s) in which he/she is participating in a situation.

register A distinction in formality of language. Not all people have access to all registers within their language.

relational orientation Productive focus is directed toward the building and maintenance of relationships, especially but not exclusively within one's own group.

salience hierarchy A rank-order list of how important things are to you.

salient categorization A stage in prejudice reduction in which more complex insights about a person from another group are generalized onto the group.

social capital The worth of networks of relationships.

stereotypes Rigid overgeneralizations, often negative.

survival intelligences An asset-based approach to understanding the unique competencies of people from difficult situations through cultural lenses.

task orientation Productive focus is directed toward accomplishing specific, identifiable objectives as opposed to relationship building.

tonal differences Variations in the pitch of sounds or words that can, in some languages or situations, change meanings. More generally, this can also refer to differences in accent.

universalism An approach to ethics that emphasizes principles of right and wrong behavior that are assumed to apply equally in all situations.

values Deeply held, unquestioned assumptions about how life works. May incorporate religious, philosophical, or other related beliefs. People generally cannot identify their own values unless they come into contact with a competing value.

word choice The process by which some words are selected for use and others are not selected. This choice can carry as much meaning as the words themselves.

Appendix A: The Intercultural Development Continuum

Through research and development of the IDI over the past decade, Hammer (2008) has released the Intercultural Development Continuum (IDC), a follow-up and corollary scale to Bennett's (1986, 1993, 1998) DMIS. As the analysis of IDI results will be conducted in reference to the IDC rather than the DMIS, the various stages of the IDC model will be considered in detail here, with reference to the DMIS as necessary for clarity.

In *Denial*, according to Bennett (2007), a person is "unable to experience differences in other than extremely simple ways" and has a worldview structure that has either "no categories or only broad categories for construing cultural difference." Furthermore "in some cases, people with this orientation may dehumanize others, assuming that different behavior is a deficiency in intelligence or personality" (p. 19). Disinterest in and avoidance of cultural difference, in Hammer's (2008) view, are featured as prominent mechanisms through which Denial plays out. The key issue to resolve in Denial, stated Bennett and Bennett (1997), is the ability to recognize the existence of culture as an explanatory principle and thus construe cultural difference.

Hammer (2008) suggested that the following stage, *Polarization*, is characterized by "a judgmental orientation grounded in a sense of 'us versus them,'" (p. 249). Bennett (2007) emphasized that in this stage it is common to have stereotyped understandings of other cultures. Polarization may either be demonstrated in Defense or Reversal. The two main variations of *Defense* are as follows: (a) Defense/Denigration, wherein any other culture (and its values and behaviors) are judged negatively; (b) Defense/Superiority, wherein positive elements of one's own culture are exaggerated (Bennett, 2007).

Bennett (2007) explained that in the other manifestation of Polarization, called Reversal, the "poles are reversed" and one views "another culture as superior while maligning one's own" (p. 20). Hammer (2008) indicated that Reversal is distinguished from Defense, because "Reversal consists of generally positive evaluations toward other cultures" (p. 249). However, he clarified by noting that both of "these evaluations are . . . stereotypic and reflect little, deeper cultural understandings of the other cultural community" (p. 249). Hammer continued that a key feature of Reversal is the tendency to be overly critical of the cultural practices of one's own group on the one hand, and uncritical of an often idealized other group on the other hand. According to Hammer, the key issue to resolve in Polarization (whether Defense or Reversal) is "to recognize the stereotypic nature of one's perceptions and experiences of the other culture and to actively identify commonalities between one's own views, needs, and goals and that of the other" (p. 249).

In Minimization attention to differences is diminished, while physical and transcendental similarities are emphasized. While Bennett (2007) conceded that this stage appears sensitive compared to the polarization of Defense, "the assumed commonality with others is typically defined in ethnocentric terms: since everyone is essentially like us, it is sufficient in cross-cultural situations to 'just be yourself'" (p. 21). Hammer (2008) noted that difference is masked by commonality lenses, such as "an over-application of human similarity, as well as universal values and principles" (p. 249). Thus the primary issue for resolution in Minimization, for Hammer, is "to deepen understanding of one's own culture (cultural self-awareness) and to increase understanding of culture general and specific frameworks for making sense (and more fully attending to) cultural differences" (p. 249).

The first truly intercultural stage of the IDC is *Acceptance*. According to Bennett (2007), individuals in acceptance "perceive that all behaviors and values, including their own, exist in distinctive cultural contexts and that patterns of behaviors and values can be discerned within each context" (p. 22). Acceptance does not indicate a blind approval of any way of approaching the world, "but rather acceptance of the distinctive reality of the other culture's worldview" (p. 22). Bennett and Bennett (1997) suggested that the primary issue for resolution in Acceptance is related to relativism that appears in two forms: behavioral and value. These forms of relativism can be experienced quite acutely and can lead to an ability to "'talk the talk' without 'walking the walk'" (Bennett, 2007, p. 22). Hammer (2008) indicated that the primary task that has to be resolved for continued movement is to "reconcile the 'relativistic' stance that aids understanding of cultural differences without giving up one's own cultural values and principles" (p. 251).

The second ethnorelative stage of the DMIS is *Adaptation*. Whereas Acceptance may be focused on cognitive processing of difference in context, with a limited ability to "walk the walk" (Bennett, 2007, p. 22), Adaptation emphasizes both cognitive frame-shifting and behavioral code-shifting. Bennett (1998) emphasized the role of empathy in Adaptation, which "describes a shift in perspective away from our own to an acknowledgement of the other person's different experience" (p. 208). Bennett (2007) stated that "the ability to empathize with another worldview in turn allows modified behavior to flow naturally from that experience. It is this natural flow of behavior that keeps code-shifting from being fake or inauthentic" (p. 23). Hammer (2008) explained that having resolved the ethical malaise of Acceptance, a person is able to deeply understand cultural difference while maintaining a strong sense of ethical commitment to other principles. It is thus that a person can accept difference without necessarily agreeing with it. The main developmental issue in Adaptation, according to Hammer, is how to "maintain an authentically competent intercultural experience—one in which substantial cognitive frame shifting and behavioral code shifting is occurring such that an individual is able to experience the world in ways that approximate the experience of the cultural 'other'" (p. 250).

Although *Integration* was considered a stage in the DMIS, the IDC has eliminated it. What is now in view is *Cultural Disengagement*, an outgrowth of Encapsulated Marginality on the DMIS in Hammer's (2008) terms, which "reflects a sense of being disconnected and not feeling fully a part of one's cultural group" (p. 251). Cultural Disengagement, he noted, can happen at various points along the IDC, but is not itself an orientation—"Cultural Disengagement is independent . . . from the procession of core orientations that comprise the intercultural development continuum" (p. 251).

Other books by Stephen W. Jones:

The Practical Interculturalist's Guidebook to Transitions Across Cultures: http://amzn.to/105WuFG

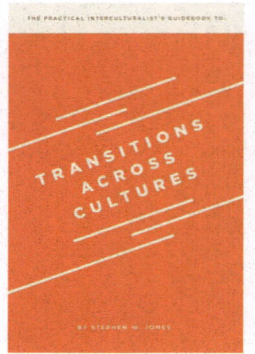

Transitions Across Cultures, the first in the Practical Interculturalist's Guidebook series, is an approachable explanation of what you can expect when crossing cultures. In this book, learn how to effectively navigate the stages of transition. Understand why you will experience culture shock and what to do about it. Identify healthy ways to deal with the stresses of crossing cultures. Prepare for returning home, whether you've been gone for a month or for years. Whether you are a first-time study-abroad student, a seasoned business traveler, or are relocating internationally, you will find this book to be very useful. Transitions Across Cultures also has advice for friends, families, and managers of those who are traveling. Includes a comprehensive glossary.

Intercultural Development in Global Service Learning: http://amzn.to/12HrefI

*This reprinting of **Intercultural Development in Global Service-Learning** makes this important research available for service-learning and study abroad practitioners. This mixed-methods study utilized the Intercultural Development Inventory (IDI v3) and in-depth student interviews to understand whether and how students experience intercultural development. Despite the small sample size, there are significant results (using the Wilcoxon signed ranks test). Iterative coding yielded three major themes, including the reasons for changes in intercultural development, the results of these changes, and the experience of those changes. These themes are fully developed in the text, and provide important information for practitioners of international education. Committee members include Eric Hartman, Peggy Pusch, and Kent Warren.*

Social Constructivism and Christianity: http://goo.gl/x2knan

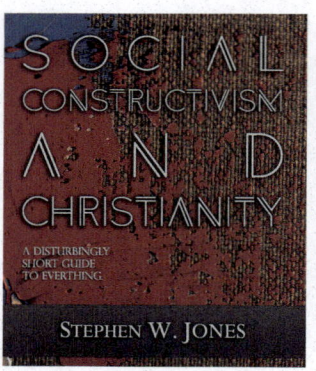

This short work attempts to find compatibility between social constructivism and biblical Christianity, without being unfaithful to either of these. Includes discussion of constructivism, reification, absolute truth, and interacting with Truth from both relational and rational cultural knowledge systems. Additionally includes a brief consideration of the religious understanding of being as viewed through evolutionary, subjective and original monotheistic positions. Concludes with the implications of social constructivism in intercultural competence and how this may be experienced by followers of Jesus. The primary audience is North American, though others may find the considerations herein to be useful and applicable to their context.

To find Jones's other writings, plan a training opportunity,

or schedule a speaking engagement,

find him at **www.thepracticalinterculturalist.com**

INDEX

CPSIA information can be obtained
at www.ICGtesting.com
Printed in the USA
LVOW01s1117310816

502221LV00005B/7/P